Rabindranath Tagore's *The Home and the World*

New Dimensions

Rabindranath Tagore's *The Home and the World*

New Dimensions

edited by

D.K. Pabby

Alpana Neogy

Asia Book Club

Published by
asia book club
New Delhi 110 058

Composed by Vivek Mathur, Delhi 110 006 Ph. 3981867
Printed at Chaman Offset Press, New Delhi 110 002

Contents

Section I
The Home and the World
Textual Analysis and Evaluation

by

D.K. Pabby and Alpana Neogy

Section II
Critical Approaches

Contributors

INDIRA BHATT	C.U. Shah College Ahmedabad
SUBHASH CHANDRA	S. Bhagat Singh College University of Delhi
RANJAN GHOSH	Viswa Bharati University Santiniketan
NOVY KAPADIA	S.G.T.B. Khalsa College University of Delhi
PRADIP LAHIRI	Nagaland University Kohima
KEYA MAJUMDAR	Jamshedpur Women's College Jamshedpur
BASAVARAJ NAIKAR	Karnatak University Dharwad
ALPANA NEOGY	R.L.A. College University of Delhi
D.K. PABBY	R.L.A. College University of Delhi
RAHUL SAPRA	S.G.T.B. Khalsa College University of Delhi
D.R. SHASHIDHARA	Mangalore University Konaje, Karnataka
NANDITA SINHA	Mata Sundari College University of Delhi
SAVITRI TRIPATHI	Govt. P.G. Arts & Com. College Bilaspur
VANASHREE TRIPATHY	Banaras Hindu University Varanasi

Introduction

D.K. PABBY and ALPANA NEOGY

Tagore: His Life and Times

The impact of Western values, thoughts and philosophies on India in the mid-nineteenth century led to the questioning of many aspects of Hindu social and religious life by the western-educated Indians. There were many Indians, however, who angrily rejected this influence. The colonisers, on the other hand, interpreted Indian values and thoughts either on purely racist lines or with thorough scholarship.

Asian wisdom and philosophy has today gained prominence all over the Western world. Yoga and meditation have become the mantra in contemporary market-driven economies. Even in the field of literature, writers who can trace their origin to the subcontinent, and for whom English is not the mother tongue, are being lauded for their insight and their command over the English language. However, it is necessary to recognise that this coming together of the East and the West is not a recent phenomenon peculiar only to recent times. In India, the East and the West have been trying to come together for a very long time.

The impact of Western thought on India in the mid-nineteenth century made many Indian thinkers veer to the realisation that it was imperative for the Hindu religion to reform to the changing times. The Hindu Reform Movement, which reached its culminating point in the 1880s, believed that the progress of India and its people could only be possible with the recognition that the oppression of women and of the lower castes must cease.

These thinkers theorized that in order to advocate equality of the sexes and the castes, universal education in India was of utmost importance.

The founding member of this Hindu Reform Movement was Raja Ram Mohun Roy (1772-1833), a Bengali Brahmin, who had been educated in Muslim schools and was as fluent in the Persian and Arabic languages as he was in Sanskrit, Bengali and English. Western thought profoundly influenced him. He criticised social practices that degraded women and although he was hostile towards the British Raj, he actively supported the British Government's decision to abolish the practice of *Sati*.

Raja Ram Mohun Roy observed that women remained oppressed and neglected in Hindu society as a result of the power differences between the two sexes. A similar power difference also existed between the upper and lower classes of the Hindu caste system. He was convinced that reform could be brought about only through education.

In 1828, Raja Ram Mohun Roy established in Calcutta the Brahmo Samaj. Initially, the members focussed on a rational study of the Vedic scriptures. Soon the members found themselves being openly critical of the Hindu practice of child marriage and of the caste system. Naturally, the orthodox Hindus were enraged.

Rabindranth Tagore (1861-1941) was born into a leading *zamindar* family of Calcutta. The family was not only one of the wealthiest families of Bengal but had been active for over two generations in the cultural movements of the times.

Dwarkanath Tagore (1794-1846), grandfather of Rabindranath, a remarkable man by any standard, was a man of many accomplishments. Critics consider him as India's first industrial entrepreneur in Calcutta, a city of merchants second only to London in the British Empire. Raja Ram Mohun Roy was his friend and Dwarkanath contributed generously to the Brahmo Samaj. A philanthropist, a leading businessman and a patron of education, Dwarkanath lived in such a lavish style in the last years of his life in Europe, that he was called "Prince Dwarkanath, the Oriental Croecus." Queen Victoria welcomed him to her Court and he entertained King Louis Phillipe at his hotel. The city of Edinburgh conferred on him the title of "The Freedom of the City." However, when he died, Dwarkanath left colossal debts behind him mainly due to failed business enterprises. Rabindranath Tagore, in his mid-life, is alleged to have destroyed his grandfather's personal correspondence, almost as though he was keen to erase the memory of the Dwarkanath story from the Tagore family itself. The family had viewed him as being too commercial in outlook and as being a toddy to the colonial powers.

Debendranth Tagore (1817-1905), son of Dwarkanath, offered to hand over the entire property to the creditors to repay his father's debts. The creditors were so impressed by this gesture that they trusted him enough to manage his estate and to pay off his father's debts at his convenience. To honour his obligations, Dwarkanath and his large family lived an austere, spartan life with a complete denial of luxury even though in reduced circumstances the annual income of the father was more than half a million rupees.

Maharshi Debendranath Tagore, as he was called, was a deeply religious man who had great faith in the Upanishads. He often went to the Himalayas to meditate, sometimes taking his fourteenth and youngest child, Rabindranath, with him. He also built a country house near Bolpur in the Birbhum district of Bengal, quite close to Calcutta, which he called Shantiniketan or Abode of Peace. The father sought to meditate at Shantiniketan. The son made this retreat world famous as the centre for his new experiments in school and university education, meaningfully called Vishwa Bharati on ideological grounds.

Debendranath became the head of the Brahmo Samaj movement. To his son Rabindranath, Raja Ram Mohun Roy was the *Bharat Pathik*, the Pathfinder of India, and he remained loyal to the principles of Brahmo Samaj throughout his life. Tagore was not opposed to Hinduism but was deeply concerned about some Hindu social practices that he felt were harmful to society. The Tagore family thus was in the forefront of the new aristocracy of Bengal in an age of extraordinary mental ferment and activity, which created new enterprises in the literary, cultural, moral, religious and political fields.

Bengali Hindu life at the turn of the nineteenth century was under the impact of three European cultural movements combined, viz., the Renaissance, the Reformation and the Romantic movement. Thus although there were many men dabbling in gardening (the water hyacinth that has choked up many a pond or lake was brought in at this time presumably from Brazil), philately and interior decoration, many more were engaged in social and religious reform, in literature, education, culture and politics. The Ramakrishna-Vivekananda Missions established by Swami Vivekananda (1863-1902), a disciple of the saint and spiritual master Sri Ramakrishna (1836-1886), could be cited as a consequence of the winds of change. Pandit Ishwar Chandra Vidyasagar (1820-91) pioneered the social and educational reforms and Madhusudan Dutta (1824-73), known as the Milton of Bengal, and Bankim Chandra Chatterjee (1838-94), known likewise as the Scott of Bengal, ushered in a fresh breath of air into the literature of Bengal.

Debendranth Tagore's family, too, tried out new professional lines. His second son became the first Indian member of the Indian Civil Service and Rabindranath was sent to England at the age of seventeen to become a barrister by passing through the Inns of Court in London. The fact that he refused to conform and was impatient of the restrictions imposed on him, is another story. Rabindranth was a romantic, yearning for the infinity and the eternity, a worshipper of freedom. He had started composing poems, plays and dance dramas from a very young age. *Bhanusingher Padavali,* influenced by Vaishnava lyrics, was written while he was a teenager.

He returned to India in 1880 without entering the Bar and gradually, with the publication of his poems, *Sandhya Sangeet* (Evening Songs), *Prabhat Sangeet* (Morning Songs), devotional songs written for the congregational chapel and others, came to be considered in Calcutta as the emerging great poet of Bengal. He was a frequent figure in the Bengali literary society. He was not yet twenty years of age as he cultivated the acquaintance of Bankim Chandra Chatterjee, the greatest contemporary literary figure of Bengal. The novel *Bou-Thakuranir Hat* (The Young Queen's Mart) was a product of this influence. His play *Prakritir Pratishodh* (Nature's Revenge) deals with the theme dear to Tagore: the polarisation between the ordinary life of feeling and sensation and the austere, harsh life of the ascetic. When the hermit comes back to the rejected, outcaste girl, he finds her dead. The ascetic learns that the noble and the great are to be found in small things.

On December 9, 1883, Tagore married the twelve year old, uneducated, daughter of one of the junior officers of the family estate. Within six months of his marriage, his favourite sister-in-law, Kadambari Devi, committed suicide. Many years later he described her as "the poet within a poet's heart" in *Chabi* (The Picture). In 1890, after failing once again to qualify for some particular profession in England, Tagore was sent by his father to manage his extensive properties in central Bengal. The main river here was the Padma, a tributary of the Ganges, and a whole network of smaller rivers flowed in or out of it.

Tagore lived for many years in this area, mostly in a houseboat, sailing from place to place, sometimes moored at a *ghat* of a village for days. And it was in this environment that he discovered himself and Bengal. Some of his best works of poetry and prose were written during this time. *Sonar Tari* (Golden Boat), one of his finest poems, the admirable collection of short stories, *Galpaguchha* (Bunch of Stories), the comedies *Baikunther Khata* (The Accounts of Baikunth) and *Chirakumar Sabha*, were written at this time. Yet he was a capable and competent landlord. Living with and observing the poor tenants of his estate, Tagore was able to understand with and have compassion for the plight of the rural poor.

On December 21, 1901, Tagore started a school with five students at Shantiniketan. A few months later, his wife, who had shared his work with him, died and Tagore was a widower at 41 years of age. Within a year, he lost his little daughter, Rani; and a son, through illness, a few years later.

In spite of these personal tragedies, Tagore continued to write. *Smaran* (Remembrance) speaks of his sorrow at this time and his volume of children's verse *Shishu* (*Crescent Moon* in the English version) reveals the genius of the master being able to overcome his sorrow.

In the world beyond Shantiniketan, political events could not be ignored. Lord Curzon in Dacca had talked about a Muslim-dominated separate province and the Partition of Bengal seemed imminent. Tagore was deeply involved and his poem *Shivaji* (1904) revealed his nationalistic emotions when his beloved Bengal was being partitioned (October 16, 1905). A boycott of British goods was announced and Tagore read a paper, *Abastha O Byabastha* ("The Situation and the Remedy") at the Calcutta Town Hall recommending the establishment of a parallel government. His songs were on everyone's lips and it was at this time that he wrote the song *Sonar Bangla* that many years later was adopted as the national anthem of Bangla Desh. Probably at this time, as he became a people's poet, he came closer to the common man than he had ever done before.

A leader of the pre-Gandhi swadeshi (self-rule) movement in Bengal, Tagore turned away from nationalist politics in disgust at the violence and the bitterness that accompanied it. He loved his country and could not accept arson and violence as being necessary or just for the sake of gaining freedom. As Nikhil, Tagore's alter ego in *The Home and the World* (Penguin Books, 1985) says: "So long as we are impervious to truth and have to be moved by some hypnotic stimulus, we must know that we lack the capacity for self-government." (42) He was often misunderstood for having turned his back to the swadeshi movement. Tagore later broke away from being actively involved in politics and concentrated in the rural upliftment of his tenants in his country estate.

It was here that he wrote *Indian Pilgrimage* wherein he enunciated that Indian culture and creativity belonged to all that belonged to India. "From the shore of her vast humanity, none will turn back or be turned back." In the play *Prayaschitta* (Atonement) Dhananjay, the ascetic spreads the message of love with his songs. The idea of *Visvamanav* or the Universal Man who would respect all religions was taking shape in his mind.

His writings now expressed his restlessness with the evils of society. The orthodox did not welcome his satire on the rigid stranglehold of society in *Achalayatan* (The Immovable Edifice) and his concern for the status of women in *Nasta Need* (The Ruined Nest), *Strir Patra* (The Wife's Letter) and *Ghare Baire* (*The Home and the World*). He wrote *Jana Gana Mana*, later adopted as the national anthem for India, for 1911 Congress session in Calcutta.

Gitanjali (1910), a collection of verses in Bengali, translated by Tagore himself, perhaps best expresses his idea of the Universal Man. The translated poems have a beauty and an appeal of their own but do not in any way approach the quality and power of the Bengali originals. Nonetheless, these poems won him the Nobel Prize for Literature in 1913. Two years later, the British Empire knighted him. In 1919, stunned by the horror of the Jallianwala Bagh massacre, Tagore renounced his title. Those who had suspected his leanings towards the Empire after he was conferred his knighthood were silenced.

Tagore's creative life of over sixty years is extraordinarily prolific. His poetry, dramas, operas, short stories, novels, essays and diaries in Bengali cover twenty-eight large volumes. His letters are contained in an equal number of smaller volumes. He composed two and a half thousand songs and his paintings and drawings exceed two thousand. Only a small fraction of his creative work has been translated.

He went on lecture tours across Europe, the Americas, China, Japan, Malaya, and Indonesia. From 1913, the year the Nobel Prize for Literature was conferred on him, Tagore denounced the excesses of nationalism not only in India but also in China, Japan and the West. Eminent poets like W.B. Yeats, Ezra Pound and contemporary leading statesmen were his friends and admirers. He died in 1941.

During his lifetime, Rabindranath Tagore was regarded as a towering and epochal figure not only within his native Bengal, or his beloved India, but throughout the world. A consummate genius, a complete renaissance man, he single-handedly transported the literature and arts of Bengal to unparalleled heights of creativity. Indian culture and the Indian psyche were revitalised by his exhilarating poems, his incomparable lyrics and by his complete support for the cause of India's freedom movement.

The Swadeshi Movement (1905-1907) and Nationalism

Rabindranath Tagore was a great admirer and friend of another colossus of the twentieth-century India, Mahatma Gandhi (1869-1948). Tagore would call Gandhi 'The Mahatma in a Peasant's Garment.' In turn Gandhi called him 'The Great Sentinel.' Yet they had their differences.

While Gandhi stressed on self-sufficiency in every walk of life, Tagore felt that it was necessary to believe in international cooperation and sharing. To Tagore, the inner swaraj and development of the self was of utmost importance.

Early in life, Tagore with his older brothers and sisters had been involved with Indian nationalism and patriotism through such family cultural functions as Swadeshi Melas (national fairs). As far back as 1877, he had stated his love for the country by attacking the Delhi Durbar in a poem.

During the last quarter of the nineteenth century, however, educated Bengali society could be divided into two groups—the liberals and the conservatives. The Brahmos and the western-educated Bengalis led the liberal movement. The Bengali conservatives school was led by Bankim Chandra Chatterjee and Swami Vivekananda who had created a revised version of Hinduism which might be called Bengali Neo-Hinduism. They, too, had a large following.

The Bengali nationalist sentiment of the conservatives was very powerful when the British government first announced the infamous Settlement in 1905 designed to partition Bengal. Strongly Hindu in their sentiment, the conservatives dominated Bengali thinking when the first active agitation against the Settlement began in 1905.

Tagore had considerable respect for the Neo-Hindu leaders and their school of thinking. He had even come under their influence and his school at Shantiniketan was based on the ancient Hindu thinking on education. In fact, he disassociated himself from the new university at Calcutta (later to become Jadavpur University in the 1950s) because his desire that it should be more Indian and less imitative of the West was ignored.

Unfortunately the majority of the educated Bengalis of the popular Hindu conservatism were crude, superstitious obscurantists. They were Hindu megalomaniacs and provincialism was their dominant quality. They were stubborn in their beliefs, totally impervious to any kind of compromise, fiercely intolerant of other faiths. They would not admit any fact that contradicted with their chauvinistic beliefs and they refused to liberate their minds. Anyone who would not subscribe to their ideology would be branded as a traitor to India. If the dissenter was a man of authority or influence, they would not hesitate to slander him.

Tagore challenged their social, political and religious superstitions and he was considered a turncoat and a heretic. Thus, though he had participated in the early days of the swadeshi movement, Tagore soon disassociated himself when he understood the true nature of the agitation leaders.

When Lord Curzon published the Proclamation for the Partition of Bengal in a gazette on 19 July 1905, a tempestuous patriotic feeling was stirred up in Bengal and Tagore was drawn into the storm. The official stand was that Partition was necessary for administrative reasons. In actual fact, the British officials, following their well-tried policy of divide and rule, were anxious to stamp out the nascent politics of Hindu Bengal. 16th October was set as the date for the Partition to come into effect.

During the month of September, Tagore composed twenty-three songs all emphasising the beauties of Bengal, and the need to revive her inner strength and greatness. These songs, expressing no hatred for the British, became extremely popular. On 16th October, Partition Day, a great crowd took to the streets singing "Banglaar Mati Banglar Jal." Tagore asked each Bengali, as a symbol of brotherhood, to tie a thread (rakhi) around the wrist of another Bengali. Tagore himself tied rakhis on the wrists of the mullahs of a mosque and some Muslim ostlers. Partition day became raksha bandhan day.

But the political aspects of the Movement did not absorb Tagore. He wanted to promote education and set up independent institutions like his school. Students of Calcutta welcomed the idea. They were ready to boycott Government schools and a crowd of young students turned up at his Calcutta home, Jorasanko, eager to leave their schools and colleges at his command. Tagore refused and they went away, angry, expressing doubts about his patriotism. In *The Home and the World*, the novel that best portrays this stage of Tagore's life, the writer has inserted a similar conflict.

Boycotts did not appeal to Tagore. He called them the anarchy of emptiness, at best a temporary measure. The Calcutta politicians were interested in inciting the villagers. Their welfare was not important to them. Tagore suggested that workers should go to the villages and through the medium of songs, dramas and magic shows, educate the villagers on sanitation and improved methods of agriculture. He wanted to talk to them about the need for proper roads, schools and water supply. This was the kind of swadeshi work that appealed to Tagore; his call fell on deaf ears.

Tagore decided to work alone on his estates. During the Swadeshi movement he set up a Benevolent Society involving 125 villages and about 70,000 people. The elected officials of the villages looked after the funds, collected partly from the estate and the rest from taxes levied. An independent judiciary system was set up to look into legal disputes. Schools and dispensaries were established, roads constructed, stagnant pools filled up and other projects to help in the distribution of water were taken up. This society remained in operation till the final partition of the country in 1947.

To Tagore, the Benevolent Society was more important than any urban enterprise. To him, the villagers were the essence of India. "If I can free only one or two villages from the bonds of ignorance and weakness, there will be built, on a tiny scale, an ideal for the whole of India" he said at his Institute for Rural Reconstruction near Shantiniketan in 1939. This is what he tried to do while he distanced himself from active politics, totally disillusioned with the Swadeshi movement. Unfortunately, he remained a misunderstood Sentinel at a time when he tried to plead for sanity.

The Home and the World: A Textual Analysis

Nikhil, the zamindar of Shukshayar in Rabindranath Tagore's novel *The Home and the World*, was an unusual landlord. He belonged to an old and dignified family that could trace its manners and customs back to the Moghul Badshahs. Yet he was absolutely modern in thought and outlook. He was the first member in his family to have pursued a college education and to have acquired a post-graduate degree. His elder brother drank himself to death, something not unusual amongst zamindar families. Since he had died without leaving any children behind him, Nikhil acquired the title of the zamindar. However, he did not drink nor was he given to any evil habits.

Nikhil, Tagore's alter ego, was unusual in many other ways. He tried to make the people of his estate produce their own requirements. He tried to invent an apparatus for extracting the juice of date trees and boiling it into sugar and treacle. It was a great success, only that the apparatus extracted more money than juice. He started a bank. Its high rate of interest (which came from his exchequer) made the village folk flock enthusiastically to the bank.

Nikhil married Bimala, a girl who the astrologers foretold would make him "an ideal wife." (17) Bimala was dark and lacked physical beauty. In fact it was for these reasons that she was accepted and loved by Nikhil's grandmother. All the earlier wives of the family, in spite of their extraordinary good looks, had failed to keep their husbands from going astray. The grandmother hoped that Bimala's ordinary looks would succeed where ravishing looks had failed. Nikhil did not disappoint her. He showered Bimala with his devotion and love and made her believe in the equality of the sexes.

Bimala had been brought up by watching her mother arrange different fruits on her father's plate, gently waving her fan to drive away the flies while he sat down for his meals—to Bimala this service was an expression of her mother's love for her husband. Nikhil, Bimala's husband, showed his love for his wife by decorating her, by giving her whatever she asked for, by educating her, but he forbade her from touching his feet in obeisance. Bimala began to think of herself as a queen, a Rani in his Rajah's house.

Nikhil lived with his grandmother and his widowed sister-in-law, both renowned for their beauty and grace. His concern for their welfare and his tendency to fulfill the often-unreasonable demands of the Bara Rani, the widowed young sister-in-law, exasperated his young wife.

Nikhil wanted his wife to come out of the purdah. Bimala was reluctant to give up her secure seclusion, content as she was with things being as they were. But he said he wanted her to be in the outside world so that she could reach her full potential. "Here you are wrapped up in me. You know neither what you have, nor what you want. . . . If we meet, and recognize each other, in the real world, then only will our love be true," (23) he told her.

When the swadeshi movement began all over Bengal, it did not leave the zamindar family unaffected. Bimala wanted to burn her foreign clothes according to the call of the swadeshis who asked Indians to destroy their foreign goods. Nikhil told her that there was no need to burn them; she just had to keep them away. His logic had failed to impress her.

Miss Gilby had been appointed to teach Bimala and there was a great flutter in the house when she arrived. Bimala, who had never bothered to find out if Miss Gilby was an Indian or a European, now tells her husband, "We must get rid of Miss Gilby." (28) He was reluctant to do so pointing out that Miss Gilby had been with them for a long while and should not be dismissed merely because she was an English lady. Bimala is temporarily won over.

One day a young boy Naren who worked in the estate insulted Miss Gilby on her way to the church. Nikhil turned him out of the house. Bimala, who was totally won over by the swadeshi movement by this time, is horrified: "There was not a single soul, that day, who could forgive my husband for that act—not even I. . . . To slander the poor boy so—and such a fine boy, too, who would forget his daily bath and food in his enthusiasm for Swadeshi," (28) she wrote in her diary. When Miss Gilby, who now decides to leave on her own accord, comes to bid her farewell, Bimala's heart would not melt. On the other hand, she felt that her husband was going too far to escort Miss Gilby to the railway station in his own carriage. And when exaggerated accounts of the incident appeared in the newspapers criticising her husband, she felt that he had been rightly served.

Nikhil's friend Sandip, a leader of the swadeshi movement, travelled all over rural Bengal preaching his brand of nationalism. Sandip and his followers came and addressed a meeting at the estate and the air echoed with the triumphant cries of Bande Mataram! Bande Mataram! Bimala's heart stirred to this call.

In the past, Bimala had seen the photographs of Sandip and had not liked what she had seen. Although he had a handsome face, she felt that there was something base about his appearance, that his eyes were not true. She also felt that he was taking advantage of her husband's friendship and goodness for she feared he gave in to his demands very easily.

When Sandip spoke that afternoon, Bimala was there to listen to him. He appeared as a man transformed. He seemed to her to be a messenger of the gods as the light of the slowly setting sun lighted up his features. Unconsciously, she pushed away the screen before her and fixed her gaze upon him. None in that crowd noticed this except Sandip whose eyes flashed full on her face just once. Bimala feels that she is no longer the lady of the Rajah's house, but the sole representative of Bengal's womanhood. And Sandip was the champion of Bengal.

Later that evening she emboldens herself to tell her husband that she would like to invite Sandip to dinner and to attend on him herself. Her husband is surprised and "he gazed at me curiously, in silence, with a look I did not quite understand." (32) In the past, she could not be persuaded when he entreated her to be present while he entertained some friends for dinner.

Bimala finds herself taking extreme care over her appearance and her wardrobe for her first meeting with Sandip. And when she meets him, he dazzles her with his charm and his air of intimacy. The opening gambit is by appealing to her emotions: "My horoscope tells me I am to die early. None of my forefathers have survived their thirtieth year. I am now twenty-seven," (34) he tells her and the dart goes home. She starts getting attracted towards the young "tragic" leader for whom "the blessings of the whole country are sure to avert the evil influence of the stars." (36)

For Nikhil everything that Sandip stands for is illogical. He cannot understand the extreme hate for everything foreign that consumed the Swadeshis. If God is to be worshipped how is it possible to hate other countries if God is present everywhere, he asks. By destroying everything foreign and by their acts of terrorism, Nikhil feels that the swadeshis were trying to pass off injustice and unrighteousness as a moral ideal.

Surprisingly it is Bimala who contradicts him. She is now completely enamoured by the popular brand of nationalism that was so abhorrent to Tagore. She says that for the good of the country she would not hesitate to snatch or filch: "I am only human. I am covetous. I would have good things for my country. . . . I have anger. I would be angry for my country's sake. . . . I would make my country a Person, and call her Mother, Goddess, Durga—for whom I would redden the earth with sacrificial offerings." (38)

As Sandip applauds her with the cry Bande Mataram, a shadow of pain passes over the face of her husband, Nikhil. He is human he says and therefore capable of performing evil deeds. He would not permit the evil in him to be exaggerated into an image of the country.

Nikhil watches helplessly as his wife is drawn away by the charismatic influence of Sandip. He understands now that when he desired that Bimala should blossom fully in her truth and power, he had forgotten to prepare himself to lay no claim over the right of possession of his wife. He also realises that perhaps Bimala regarded propriety and decency as a lack of forcefulness. She loved to find in men the turbulent, the angry, and the boisterous. He himself had become unpopular because he had not joined his countrymen in their "carousals." (42) And he was vilified because he kept his own counsel, accused either for longing for some title from the British Government or of being afraid of the police. The police, too, suspected him for harbouring some terrorists, as he was so mild in his dealings.

For the nationalist Sandip, this is a sign of impotence. "My country does not become mine simply because it is the country of my birth. It becomes mine on the day when I am able to win it by force," (45) he believes. He is never ashamed to take whatever he wants. To Sandip, people like Nikhil have only an obsession to die, they live in an idealistic world of lotus-eaters. They deal with words, not realities.

He is ruled by a "masterful passion" (48) quite unlike the dried, ascetic quality that he finds in Nikhil. And it is this "indomitable passion" which sweeps away everything "on the flood-tide . . . recking naught as to whether it takes them to life or to death" (48) that women find so attractive in him. Women, too, he feels know that it is this invincible emotion that is the lifeblood of the world. Therefore, he reasons, if Bimala has found that affinity with him (and not with her husband) why should he allow the fact that she was his friend's wife come in the way?

The exposure to the outside world turns Bimala's life upside down. Till now her life had been like a small river at the border of a village. Now she can hardly recognise her former self. She is intoxicated by Sandip's pleas that she should free her powers from performing "petty household duties" veiled in a zenana. Sandips's hungry eyes, full of worship, make Bimala feel that she was a wonder in beauty and power.

He calls her his Queen Bee. She feels within herself divine strength, the splendour of Bengal. He would consult her on every little thing related to the cause of swadeshi and he would receive her suggestions in raptures. Her husband, of course, had no place in their counsels, often treated as a younger brother, of whom personally one may be very fond of and yet have no use for. Thus, without her even being aware of it, Sandip gradually alienates her from her husband who had been her idol in the nine years of her married life.

Bimala now looks for opportunities to be alone with Sandip. No longer does she think it necessary for her to have her husband around for the sake of propriety when she meets Sandip. She would surreptitiously go to the library and make appropriate noises there so that Sandip would know that she was in the next room, waiting to meet him.

The Bara Rani, a constant thorn on the flesh of Bimala, had been watching the events with alarm. She had never hesitated to remark on the changes that she saw in the Chota Rani, Bimala. Her words of caution had been considered by Bimala as signs of a jealous woman, not of a woman alarmed at the path chosen by Bimala.

When things seem to be going out of hand, Bara Rani intervenes. She orders her guard, Nanku, to stop Sandip from entering the library where Bimala awaited him. Sandip refuses to take orders from a servant, and tries to enter the library. Nanku, takes him by the arm and says, "No, sir, you must not." The response from Sandip, the nationalist totally committed to freeing his country from foreign rule that suppressed the common man, is amazing. "What! To be touched by a flunkey! I snatched away my arm and gave the man a sounding blow." (53) Bimala is outraged to learn that someone had tried to issue orders that prevented her from meeting Sandip and that a servant should dare to insult him. She demands that Nanku be dismissed; she cannot do anything about her sister-in-law, after all, but tolerate her constant jibes. Her husband quietly relocates Nanku to another part of the estate. The servant had merely been following "orders." Bimala considers that in the battle for control between her and Bara Rani, her husband had failed to ensure her supremacy in the household.

Nikhil watches his wife getting ensnared in the web laid out by Sandip for whom any act, no matter how cruel it may be, is acceptable for "the cause of the country." He does not intervene or rebuke her for he feels she had to see the truth by herself. As he remains "voiceless," (85) he wonders "why cannot I sing? . . . My life has only its dumb depths; but no murmuring rush." (85)

And then comes the great revelation. So long as he continued to suffer, Bimala would never have true freedom. He must free her completely. Otherwise he himself would not be freed from the untruth. He notices certain signs of neglect: the flowers that she would place before his picture are fresh no longer. And his photograph placed on her table has an accompanying photograph: Sandip's.

Panchu, the tenant of a neighbouring zamindar, is brought in as a contrast to emphasise Tagore's appreciation and sympathy for the economically backward classes. Panchu was extremely poor and had been introduced to Nikhil through his master, Chandranath Babu. One day Panchu came and gave Nikhil a basketful of coconuts. They were being given to "pay back" for the ones he had stolen from Nikhil's garden when he was hard pressed. Nikhil's own houseguest, Sandip, had no such qualms or awareness of the rules of hospitality. The fact that he was virtually destroying the marriage of his hosts was of no consideration to him.

Nikhil believed that those who compel others to make sacrifices in the name of the country are her enemies. Such people would deny freedom to others in order that they reached the top. He himself did not hesitate to use indigenously made knives and pens and drank water from a bell metal vessel. And he did not insist that all should follow his example. But his brand of swadeshi did not appeal to anyone barring the Bara Rani who saw no harm in encouraging him as she simply cannot bear "as you can, the sight of the smile leaving his face" (96) she tells Bimala. Bimala, on the other hand, is intoxicated with the conviction that she is Shakti, possessing divine power. Nothing can fetter her—nothing was impossible for her.

As part of the Swadeshi movement in Bengal, youths from schools and colleges give up their studies and join the movement. One such boy is Amulya, as completely devoted to Bimala as he is to the cause. These young students tell Nikhil to ban foreign goods from his market. It is Nikhil's master, Chandranath Babu, visiting him at this time, who replies that when one refers to one's country, one does not mean the soil but the people in it. What would the poor traders eat, what would they wear if their means of livelihood were taken away from them? The poor always remained poor, misused by the rich and the powerful as a tool to further their own ends. To bring out man from obscurity to light should be man's highest aim, he tells them.

The youngsters go back, shame-faced. Bimala now attempts to influence her husband convinced that she would succeed where all else had failed. She attires herself in her finery, redecorates her room with flowers and sends for her husband. He immediately sees through her charade and tells her that if he orders his tenants to ban foreign goods, this would tantamount to tyranny and he would never stoop so low. Her adornments, which in the past had seemed to be part of her personality, now appear cheap and marketable.

Now Nikhil is able to view his wife dispassionately and this awareness is a freedom from the "broken cage." He had been living in a "false paradise of illusion" (111) till now. She, on her part, is astonished and humiliated at being refused a request by her husband who had till now fulfilled her every whim.

Events move fast thereafter. When he finds the villagers resisting his call for the ban of foreign goods, Sandip asks his followers to set fire to all the goods of the villagers. The boatman Mirjan was still insubordinate. Young Amulya is asked to go after dusk and arrange to load Mirjan's boat with rubbish, holed, and set adrift. It sank mid-stream. Mirjan understands the message and comes and asks Sandip for a compensation of two thousand rupees. Sandip now realises that the movement can make no headway unless he lays his hands on plenty of money.

He asks Bimala, his Queen Bee, for fifty thousand rupees, not by selling off her jewellery but from her husband's treasury. His money was hers, the country's, whom he had deprived in the time of its need, he tells her. The police have to be bribed and hush-money paid. "Underneath the cult of Bande Mataram, as indeed at the bottom of all mundane affairs, there is a region of slime, whose absorbing power must be reckoned with," (119) he tells her making her believe that the lesser wants form a part of the wants of thc great cause.

Bimala promises to give Sandip the fifty thousand rupees. How to get it, where to get it, were minor points not worth troubling over: "Look at me. Had I not risen, all in one moment, from my nothingness to a height above everything? So shall all things come at my beck and call. I shall get it, get it, get it—there cannot be any doubt . . . how, I do not care; for sin there cannot be. Sin only taints the weak; I with my Shakti am beyond its reach." (138).

So Bimala believes. Only a commoner can be a thief. She is so intoxicated by the spell of Sandip that she really believes that taking the money from her husband's treasury is not theft but mere taking of the "rightful spoil."

She sends for her devoted disciple Amulya to ask him if he could get the money out of the treasury for the cause. He was prepared to do anything for her, he says. She then asks him how he proposed to go about getting the money as the treasury was so well guarded. Amulya fumbled in the pocket of his tunic and pulled out, first a small edition of the *Gita* and then a little pistol.

Bimala is now struck with horror. It did not take Amulya a moment to make up his mind to kill the good old cashier. The cashier's place in the world meant nothing real to him. And when she protests against the need to kill the cashier pleading that the man had a wife and children, she is further alarmed to hear him echo the platitudes of Sandip: "Look here, Maharani, the thing we call pity is, at bottom, only pity for ourselves. We cannot bear to wound our own tender instincts, and so we do not strike at all—pity indeed! The height of cowardice!" (139)

It is here and now that Bimala sees reality. "The Mother in me awoke." (139) She is staggered to hear Sandip's phrases in the mouth of this "delightfully, lovably immature" boy. He belonged to that age group that should believe in the existence of goodness, a time when one really lives and grows. She apprehends that Sandip's influence on the young Amulya had wrought the demise of everything that was beautiful and just in the young boy.

Bimala is now determined to save Amulya who, with no sin in his heart, calmly talked of murdering the inoffensive old man as though it was the right thing to do. No longer is she concerned about her power. Now she is the Mother, wanting to give and save life, ready to stave off the devil's progress.

Bimala decides that she must act on her own. Every year her husband made a reverence offering of six thousand rupees to his sister-in-law at the time of Durga Puja. This money was kept in the iron safe in Bimala's dressing room before it was deposited in a bank at Calcutta. Nikhil would leave the keys to the iron safe in his pocket when he took off his clothes for the night. Bimala takes the key of the safe and on opening it finds the money, not in currency notes, but in gold rolled up in paper. She ties the gold sovereigns to the corner of her sari and feels: "What a weight it was. The burden of the theft crushed my heart to the dust. Perhaps notes would have made it seem less like thieving, but this was all gold." (144)

She tries to enthuse herself by chanting Bande Mataram, Bande Mataram so that she could feel that for the sake of the country she had a right over the money. But there was an overwhelming sense of shame not of glory: "I could not think of my house as separate from my country: I had robbed my house, I had robbed my country. For this sin my house had ceased to be mine, my country also was estranged from me. Had I died begging for my country, even unsuccessfully, that would have been worship, acceptable to the gods." (144)

She now comprehends that she had been swept away by her folly and pride. She also understands that she had put her foot on quicksand and could not withdraw it. When the gold coins wrapped in paper are handed over to Sandip, thinking them to be mere paper, his face grew black. "Is that all?" (147) he asks totally oblivious of the mental torture that had gone behind the theft. Bimala is humiliated, as she now knows that she had been a mere pawn in the hands of Sandip, ever ready to do his bidding. When he sees the gold, he pays obeisance to Bimala and addresses her as "goddess." Bimala is once again enchanted. Her theft seems to gain a dignity and all stings of conscience are wiped away.

Yet when she is at home, shame engulfs her. She is ashamed to even sit near her husband. She prepares to pawn all her jewels to replace the stolen six thousand rupees even though her jewels are worth more than five times that amount. Amulya comes in to tell her how ashamed he was that his Sister Rani, as he calls Bimala, was mortified. He wanted the money to be returned but Sandip had no regrets or compunctions about taking the money. For the magic of Bande Mataram, Sandip said, one must get rid of the idea that the money belonged to the one in whose box it happened to be.

Bimala now decides that even though she may have to die in the process, she must wean Amulya away from the snake Sandip and save him. She gives him her jewel-box with the instruction that it should be concealed from Sandip, and the stolen money recovered.

The nationalist movement to which Sandip belonged believed that Muslims must know their place and remain suppressed so that they never forgot that the Hindus were their masters. Nikhil was quite upset at this form of nationalism as there were both Hindus and Muslims living amicably in his estate for generations. He knows that fanaticism is at the bottom of this kind of propaganda and that this would only lead to the degeneration of the country. To Nikhil, Muslims were a necessary part of India and he asks Sandip not to harass and oppress his tenants any longer but to leave his territory.

"True patriotism will never be roused in our countrymen unless they can visualize the motherland. We must make a goddess of her," (120) Sandip proposes next. He is determined to make his country have a divine image. "Divinities are set up in every country to keep up the illusions of the people, for men are only too well aware of their weakness," he reasons. The Brahmins will be appointed as priests of this goddess and Bimala's image will be installed in the temples. She will become an image of worship from which none can withhold belief for she would represent Divine Mother. Nikhil protests saying that one should not seek the help of illusions. Sandip remarks smugly, "Who says 'Truth shall triumph'? Delusion shall win in the end" (125).

Sandip's strong Hindu fanatical speeches and actions soon recoil on him. He is warned about Muslim preachers getting ready to attack him. The Muslims in Nikhil's estate had as much aversion for cow killing as the Hindus but now cases of cow killings are reported. Nikhil calls his Hindu tenants and speaks to them about restraint and tolerance. An English-knowing tenant remarks that the Muslims have taken the law in their own hands because they are assured of safety even if they break the law, a reference, of course, to the divide and rule policy made famous by the British colonial power. Nikhil lays the blame for the Hindu-Muslim divide right where it should be laid. "Why is it possible," I asked, "to use the Mussulmans thus, as tools against us (the Hindus)? Is it not because we have fashioned them into such with our own intolerance?" (162)

But his is a voice in the wilderness. As the news of his "notorious" (162) stand spreads over the countryside, his effigy is burnt in the cremation grounds. Nikhil now receives letters written in blood and cartoons and lampoons appear in newspapers ridiculing him. Freedom cannot be brought about by downright oppression and by instilling fear amongst the weaker sections of society and the minorities, he believes.

Nikhil simultaneously concludes that he himself would never be free till he set his wife free.

> "Bimala," said I, "why should I seek to keep you fast in this closed cage of mine? Do I not know that thus you cannot but pine and droop?"

She stood still, without raising her eyes or uttering a word.

"I know," I continued, "that if I insist on keeping you shackled my whole life will be reduced to nothing but an iron chain. What pleasure can that be to me?"

She was still silent.

"So," I concluded, "I tell you, truly, Bimala, you are free. Whatever I may or may not have been to you, I refuse to be your fetters." (133-34)

To Nikhil freedom of thought is the biggest gift of man. Nothing could be compared to it. He could not keep his wife in bondage as that would mean "to clutch hold of that which is untrue as though it were true." (134) It is because of his belief in personal freedom that he finds it so difficult to accept the objectives of the swadeshis. They believe in coercion, in keeping their followers in shackles, in setting limits to the mind of man. In the process these people had been spreading a "thousand-and-one snares—of religion, custom and selfishness." The country needed to be saved from this form of treachery. "I cannot let the country go to rack and ruin even if that would please everybody," (163) he sighs as he watches helplessly.

The Chakna sub-treasury is looted of six thousand of the seven thousand rupees in the safe by an armed band. Kasim, the guard is wounded. Kasim is arrested but Nikhil refuses to believe him to be the guilty one.

Bimala had asked Amulya to sell her jewels to replenish the Bara Rani's Durga Puja remittance. Now it dawns on her that Amulya was much too young to have been commissioned for such a task. She fears his arrest for which she would hold herself responsible. Exposure and public humiliation would definitely follow. "Bara Rani whom I have so long despised" (167) will have her revenge she fears.

Now the sight of Sandip disgusts and nauseates her. How well she had been manipulated like a puppet on a string! He startles her by taking out her jewel casket from the folds of his cloak when he meets her. Her immediate reaction is relief—Amulya had not gone to Calcutta after all! Sandip would like to believe that she was relieved to see her jewels were safe! In sheer disgust, she tells him, "If they [the jewels] have exerted your greed, you may have them." (169)

Amulya, hair tumbled, lips dry, "the freshness of his youth . . . withered in a single day" (169) rushes in. He had wanted to return the jewels to Bimala but had been forestalled by Sandip who had stolen the jewel-box from his trunk. But Bimala is not interested in her jewels any more. "Let him who hankers after them, satisfy his greed," (169) she soothes him. But Amulya would have none of it and he challenges Sandip who now completely changes his tune: "I did not come here today to take these jewels, I came to give them to you. You would have done wrong to take my gift at Amulya's hands. In order to prevent it, I had first to make them clearly mine. Now these my jewels are my gift to you. Here they are!" (170)

He knows now that Bimala is sick of the sight of him, that his hold on her has waned but he is not willing to accept defeat graciously. If anyone, it is Amulya who has brought about his downfall and so he tells him to pack his suitcase and leave the room he shared with him.

After Sandip departs, Amulya takes out six thousand rupees in currency notes, as he could not get the amount in gold. He admits that he had obtained the amount "wrongly." (171) Bimala now grasps the magnitude of her crime. In her desperate attempt to put back the money that she had stolen from her husband, Amulya too had been dragged into the quagmire. "It was an evil moment when you first came to me. Even Sandip has not been able to harm you as I have done," (171) she regrets. "To sin is easy enough, but to make up for it is above all difficult for a woman. . . . My hardest punishment is that I must put on you the burden of my sin." (181)

Bimala asks Amulya to put the money back where he had found it. He tells her that that would be impossible. She insists as she feels that this is the only way by which both of them could rid themselves of the evil spell of Sandip.

Later she hears from Bara Rani that six thousand rupees

had been stolen from the family treasury. Bimala's first reaction was to call Amulya back. He need not return the money. Difficult though it was, she would explain matters to her husband, declare that she was at the bottom of the robbery.

But even this confession becomes difficult. She feels that she had converted all the wealth that had been given to her into her burden. She is far away from all those who are around her. She is alone, with no companion. Her heart breaks, as she knows that she herself has made her life so turbulent. She wishes she could die as she throws herself on the ground, weeping. Just then she hears the footsteps of her husband. "Come, oh come, come and let your feet touch my head. Come, Lord, and set your foot upon my throbbing heart, and at that moment let me die," (186) her heart cries out. He strokes her head. She receives his blessing. Now she would be able to take up the penalty of public humiliation which would be hers. But she also knows that the destruction and havoc created in her relationship with her husband is virtually irreversible.

Nikhil had been woken from his sleep by a deep moaning sound of someone sobbing from the heart. He goes to the balcony. It is Bimala. He almost returns to his room but he cannot. He sits down on the ground near Bimala and places his hand on her head. Both of them have drifted apart so much that they cannot even confide in each other. "My union with you, my love, was only of the wayside; it was well enough so long as we followed the same road; it will only hamper us if we try to preserve it further," (187) he writes in his diary.

The master, Chandranath Babu, who had been watching and drawing his own conclusions, now suggests that Sandip should be asked to leave and Bimala be taken away to Calcutta. "She is getting too narrow a view of the outside world from here, she cannot see men and things in their true proportions. Let her see the world—men and their work—give her a broad vision," (165) he counsels.

The Police Inspector arrives with Amulya and the six thousand rupees he had stolen from the treasury. Amulya refuses to tell where the money had come from. He is suspected of shielding the thief and to Nikhil he says, "It was I, by myself, alone." (193) But when he is asked why he stole and then tried to return the money, he answers, "Let her come, at whose command I did so. In her presence I shall make a clean breast of it . . . my sister, the Chota Rani!"

When she arrives, Amulya prostrates himself in salutation and takes the dust of her feet. He had executed her command and returned the money, he says. With her image in mind, he had not uttered a single lie. He has cast away the watchword Bande Mataram and he awaited her blessing.

Bimala's reply, "You have saved me, my little brother," (194) is an eye-opener for Nikhil: "I could only preach and preach . . . and get my effigy burnt for my pains. I had not yet been able to bring back a single soul from the path of death. They who have the power, can do so by a mere sign. My words have not that ineffable meaning. I am not a flame, only a black coal, which has gone out. I can light no lamp." (194)

The key to the iron safe is found to be missing from the ring. Bimala admits she had it with her. She had taken out the money and spent it, she says. Nikhil suspects that there was some connection between the taking of this six thousand from the iron safe and the robbing of the other from the treasury but he refrains from asking her any questions.

He wallows in self-introspection instead. It had been his constant dream to draw his dearly loved Bimala in his work of creating himself. When he most needed a helpmate, he was alone, and would remain so till the end of his life, as she had not received the "vital spark" that he had received. Perhaps, he ponders, he was a despot in his desire to mould Bimala and she had to steal the money because she could not be open with him. "It is our unyielding obstinacy, which drives even the simplest to tortuous ways. In trying to manufacture a helpmate, we spoil a wife," (198) he reasons with great insight.

Nikhil concludes that it was wrong of him to "fetter" his life's companion with his ideas. She should have been allowed to grow true to herself. Too much time had been lost in misunderstanding and wounds must be bandaged. He takes Bimala by the hand and leads her into the room. She breaks into tears, he says nothing. She kneels at his feet, touching them repeatedly with her head, in obeisance. He tries to stop her, in a choking voice she says, "No, no, no, you must not take away your feet. Let me do my worship." (199)

There is joy in Bimala's heart as she and her husband get ready to go to Calcutta. She has passed through fire and "what was inflammable has been burnt to ashes; what is left is deathless. I have dedicated myself to the feet of him, who has received all my sin into the depths of his own pain." (199)

Nikhil comes forward to give her a hand in the packing saying that he was miserable if he was not in her company. Sandip arrives and places on the table the stolen sovereigns tied in his handkerchief. It is not Nikhil's company that has suddenly turned him honest. But it is the influence of Bimala, her purity and her devotion, that has wrought this change. "After all these days, Queen Bee, the ghost of compunction has found an entry into my hitherto untroubled conscience. As I have to wrestle with it every night, after my first sleep is over, I cannot call it a phantom of my imagination. There is no escape even for me till its debt is paid. Into the hands of that spirit, therefore, let me make restitution. Goddess! From you, alone, of all the world, I shall not be able to take away anything. I shall not be rid of you till I am destitute. Take these back!" (200)

He also takes out the jewel-casket from under his tunic and hurriedly leaves the room saying that to the Muslims he was an "invaluable gem," (201) and that they were conspiring to loot him and hide him away in their graveyard. This is a changed Sandip—changed by his contact with Bimala—who now says that he has no intention to die and must rush to catch a north-bound train to Calcutta.

Chandranath Babu, the master, enters to say that the Muslims were looting the treasury of Harish Kundu, the neighbouring zamindar, and violating the honour of the women of the house.

"I am off," (201) says Nikhil and gallops away on a horseback, with not a weapon in his hand. Bimala tries to stop him but he asks her not to be alarmed. The Bara Rani comes in and chides her for her inability to hold her husband back and she orders the Dewan to send a mounted man to bring back the Maharaja at once. If he should refuse to return he should be told that the Bara Rani was on her deathbed, she instructs him. Her anger is then turned on the hapless Bimala, "Oh, you witch, you ogress, you could not die yourself, but needs must send him to his death," (202) she cries.

Bimala watches in silence. Throughout the day she keeps a vigil by the window awaiting her fate. The Bara Rani prays but Bimala could not move a step from the window. So long as she was alive her sin would remain rampant, scattering destruction on every side, she thinks and believes that if she could die, all this turmoil would come to an end.

Late at night, a group of lights appear in the distance and a great crowd wound its way in the darkness towards the palace gates. A palanquin is followed by a litter. The doctor walks alongside the palanquin. Bimala overhears the doctor speaking to the Dewan. Nikhil has a serious wound in the head. He can't say yet about his chances of survival. And Amulya had been done for. A bullet had gone through his heart.

An Assessment of the Novel

The Home and the World (1915) is written in the form of monologues or *atmakathas*. The three main characters in the novel, Nikhil, Bimala and Sandip, record events and their innermost thoughts from their individual perspectives. In the process, the plot develops, characters grow and a denouement is reached that eventually releases the tension in the novel.

The Home and the World follows the traditional triangular relationship pattern so often found in Tagore's works. Bimala, married to the austere Nikhil, is attracted to Sandip, his nationalist friend. Eventually good sense prevails and she draws back just in time. By then, however, Nikhil is seriously wounded, Amulya (her young devotee responsible for opening her eyes) is killed and Sandip flees as he does not want to face the havoc that he has created.

All the three monologues are inter-connected and mesh into each other. Consequently, the reader gets a complete viewpoint, denied to the three main characters in the novel. When Bimala turns against Sandip and his swadeshi movement, the reader is aware of her change of heart, her agony and her sense of guilt for having stolen money, much before her husband Nikhil is aware of the change.

Bimala had fried cakes and kept them ready for Amulya who had been sent by her to return to the treasury the six thousand rupees he had initially stolen for Bimala. She keeps a vigil for Amulya the whole day waiting to feed him the cakes as *prasad*. Fear grips her as she wonders if perhaps she had sent him to his death.

When the Police Inspector arrives with a thief, Bara Rani sends down some of the cakes for the Inspector. It is Nikhil who instructs that some cakes should be sent down for the thief, too, who perhaps needed to be refreshed much more. Little did he know that the thief was none other than Amulya. Nor did he know that Bimala had made the cakes for Amulya alone and that she was responsible for turning him into a "thief." Nikhil's ignorance adds a sense of irony and pathos to the entire scene.

With extreme skill, Tagore conveys a change, an awakening in all the three diarists, Bimala, Sandip and Nikhil. They are not static but vibrant characters expressing their agonies, their doubts, their conflicts and complexes through their writings. The instrument for change is not the same in each case, however. For Bimala, the catalyst is young Amulya while she herself awakens Sandip and Nikhil to reality.

Bimala's *atmakatha* differs from the other two in more ways than one. It is written *after* the main events in the novel are over. There is a look-back factor in her diary. She assesses and evaluates events, and she expresses regret for most of her actions. This analysis is not present in the other two diarists. They write of events as they occur without any retrospection.

Bimala's *atmakatha* is addressed to her mother, in the form of an expiation of her guilt. She hopes that her mother would understand and forgive her. Bimala regrets that she had been dazzled by the patriotic jingoism of Sandip. She had failed to realise that he had been using her. Unlike Sandip the manipulator, she herself was sincere about her devotion to the cause and had believed him.

Physically she was not a beauty, she says, yet her husband, Nikhil, a zamindar, surprised her by selecting her as his bride. She had been accustomed to watch her mother perform acts of self-denial for her husband. This, to her, was an expression of her mother's love for her husband. This was the world she was accustomed to.

Nikhil wanted his wife, Bimala, by his side as an equal, not have her touch his feet in obeisance at dawn, as Bengali women were wont to do. He wished to educate her, to make her come out of the zenana, to see the world outside. This "education" was totally new to Bimala. She had to mentally readjust herself to a new environment and exposure.

While she experiences something so novel in her life—meeting for the first time a dynamic, flashy young man who was not her husband, feeling the importance of *doing* something worthwhile for the sake of the country—there is no one with whom Bimala is able to interact. Nikhil's grandmother, who loved her, is no more and Bara Rani, the only other woman in the household, is no friend of hers for she never lets a moment go by without passing some unpleasant jibes. Her husband is never her confidante.

For Bimala, it is young Amulya, not her silent, austere husband who brings about an awakening from the dizzy world of Sandip's Bande Mataram which had virtually reduced her to being a thief in her own home. She is aware that her support for the movement was creating tensions within her home, that her husband was unhappy. Yet this does not in any way stop her from meeting Sandip and being affected by his nationalistic rhetoric. Nothing seems to touch her as she slides headlong into treachery, neither her conscience nor the taunts of the Bara Rani. She is so convinced of the rightness of her actions, that she really believes that even theft for the sake of the country is right.

When Amulya, the young student, enters her life, all her maternal instincts, suppressed during the last nine years of her marriage, come to the fore. She is completely enchanted by his innocence and immaturity and when she hears him spouting nationalistic phrases (he merely echoes Sandip) and is ready to kill for the sake of the cause, it is then that her eyes are opened. She feels that his youth, a time of learning and growth was being exploited and misdirected to a path of violence and terrorism. Like a true mother, she vows to save him from destruction.

Sandip is now regarded with aversion and disgust, a schemer against whose influence she must protect Amulya. Her faith in the swadeshi movement disappears and even the call of Bande Mataram seems hollow.

Sandip, the fiery nationalist, who had made violence and terrorism the credo of his life, is not shown as a man without a conscience. Although at the beginning he has no compunction in playing with the affections of his friend's wife, we see a different man near the end of the novel. At the beginning, Sandip is all fire and rhetoric. For the sake of the cause, he is willing to exploit, to burn, to destroy. With his oratorical skills and charismatic looks, he is able to arouse passion amongst his followers who are prepared to do anything he bids them to do. Sandip, however, takes care to see that he is never the one to commit the crime.

Bimala is bewitched by his seductive appeal. He flatters her into believing that she is the Queen Bee without whose blessings the movement could not move forward. Sandip tells her that the money in her husband's treasury is her money, the country's money, and she believes him. She steals six thousand rupees, and when he acclaims her as the goddess of the cause, all sense of guilt and shame that had consumed her, abruptly vanish. She is even willing to hand over to him her casket of jewels.

Yet even this cold, calculating, manipulative Sandip has a conscience and undergoes a change of heart. When the Muslims, alienated by Sandip's brand of nationalism, start rioting and baying for his blood, Sandip decides to flee to Calcutta. But he cannot leave till he has cleared his "debts," made restitution for his sins.

His conscience is not awakened by the awareness that he had been dallying with the affections of a married woman, the wife of his friend who was also his host. Yet he is changed by none other than Bimala herself when he comprehends the enormity of her sacrifice and the depth of her love for the country. She was prepared to forego the love of her husband and the security of her home for the sake of the cause. Her commitment to save Amulya from the evils of nationalism was just as strong as her devotion to her husband and home. She was the superior being, the shakti in every sense of the word. He returns to her the stolen money and the casket of jewels saying, "Goddess! From you, alone, of all the world, I shall not be able to take away anything. I shall not be rid of you till I am destitute." (200)

Nikhil, like Sandip, may be accused of virtually making Bimala his experimental tool, someone on whom he could try out his various theories and philosophies. Sandip weaves a spell around Bimala to see how far she would go for the sake of Bande Mataram. Her husband, Nikhil, too, exposes her to the world outside without either preparing her for it or providing her with the support she needs in her moments of torment and doubt.

Undoubtedly, Nikhil's intentions were noble—he wanted to educate her, to make her see the world, to come out of the zenana. But one cannot help but feel that at the crucial time when she needed guidance from him, he failed her. After living in seclusion for so long, it was but natural for Bimala to be dazzled by the outside world.

Nikhil has a philosophic bent of mind and is a complete contrast to his fiery, jingoistic friend, Sandip. Nikhil loves his wife deeply yet self-pride is a very important factor in their relationship. He is a proud zamindar and, therefore, certain things are *infra dig*. He never questions his wife, for example, when she decides to do anything out of the ordinary.

Nikhil watches as Sandip charms his wife. He never interferes or tries to hold her back. It is the Bara Rani who makes every attempt to obstruct the development of this alarming intimacy. Instead, Nikhil resolves to free her from his shackles because "my life will be reduced to nothing but an iron chain. What pleasure can that be to me?" Does his desire to "free Bimala" stem from a consideration of her welfare? Did he really consider her true desire when he tells her that he would like to free her? There is no record of the husband and the wife ever discussing the deteriorating aspect of their relationship. They debate about the country, about swadeshi instead. "My trial is hard indeed. Just when I want a helpmate most, I am thrown back on myself alone," (197) he laments, a trifle selfishly, forgetting that he himself had not been much of a "helpmate" himself.

It required his master Chandranath Babu to suggest the obvious. Bimala should be taken to Calcutta. She required a change of scene. "She is getting too narrow a view of the outside world from here, she cannot see men and things in their true proportions. Let her see the world—men and their work—give her a broad vision," (165) he advises. It is small wonder that with this tunnel vision that Bimala had, she initially chose to follow Sandip.

Bimala steals six thousand rupees for the cause. She finds it difficult to confess to her husband. She repents and is full of guilt. Her husband has no inkling of the storm that is raging within her. She is traumatised by a sense of the harm she feels she had done to Amulya. As Nikhil himself confesses, "She has had to steal this six thousand rupees because she could not be open with me, because she felt that, in certain things, I despotically differed from her." (198)

Ultimately, it is Bimala who makes him understand the meaning of sacrifice and devotion and about putting of others' welfare before one's own. He sees how important Amulya and the country is to his wife when she comes forward and admits that she had initially taken the money, and that she had instructed Amulya to replace the stolen money to the treasury. Her biggest regret, she says, is that for her sake Amulya had to risk his life. Had she not been a woman, she laments, she would have undertaken the task herself and not exposed Amulya to so much risk. For the sake of the welfare of her country and its people, no sacrifice is big enough for Bimala.

Amulya tells her that he has abandoned Nikhil's watchword Bande Mataram. Now Bimala's image is firmly established in his mind. It is this image that commands him now to always speak the truth. Hearing this, Nikhil confesses that he could only "preach and preach," (194) but the real change in Amulya has been brought about by Bimala. By living in his ivory tower, wrapped in idealism, he had not yet been able to bring back a single soul from "the path of death." (194) Unlike Nikhil, Bimala changed others because she dared to meet life, not through speeches or speculations but through action and sacrifice. She herself was singed in the process but she came out of the flames, a phoenix reborn.

Perhaps it was this realisation, the need to act, the need to think of the other before one's own self, which makes Nikhil say, "I am off," (201) and to go out to quell the riots which had broken out in the neighbouring farm at the end of the novel. He is carried home with a serious wound in the head. Perhaps the head injury is symbolic of his first brush with harsh reality. All this while, he had been cogitating and contemplating with hardly any action resulting from his thoughts. He had been following his intellect instead of listening to his heart.

Tagore had a clear idea of the path that Indians must choose to achieve the well being of his beloved land. In *The Home and the World*, he conveys his message to his fellow Indians. In the three protagonists, Sandip, Nikhil and Bimala, Tagore represents three different approaches to reach the goal of a free, prosperous and just India. At the end of the novel, the reader is left in no doubt as to the approach that Tagore wanted his countrymen to adopt. It is not the path of aggressive revolution as typified by Sandip, nor is it a withdrawal into thoughts, paralysing all action that Nikhil portrays. Instead, it is the Mother Goddess, nurturing, sacrificing and gentle who, in the form of Bimala, shows the chosen path. She transforms all who come in contact with her. She brings redemption to the one sworn to self-seeking violence, she stirs the ivory tower dweller, Nikhil to stirring action and she rescues Amulya's innocence.

Sandip is the rebel, the nationalist, convinced that India's problems would be solved once the British left her shores. Nationalists, like Sandip, believed that India's miseries, her shortcomings, her helplessness were due to successive invasions. Political freedom, they argued, would automatically bring about social freedom and justice for all. They did not see any inadequacies in the Indian social fabric that needed correction before the rank and file of Indian society could be free.

The shortsightedness of their approach is evident in the novel. Sandip orders his followers to destroy the goods of all those who were resisting the swadeshi movement. When the victims started demanding compensation, when the Muslims began to riot because of the Hindu coercion, when the entire movement degenerated into a Hindu-Muslim problem, Sandip realises the folly of his ways. He flees the scene, having accomplished nothing.

Nikhil, the scholar and the thinker, believes that the problem is not political but social. He tackles the problem at the grass-root level. He tries to alleviate the sufferings of his tenants by opening up rural banks and by introducing scientific methods of farming. His methods involve a drain on his exchequer and achieve some benefits of a transient nature. However, when Sandip's disruptive and divisive politics fire communal passions, Nikhil is helpless in holding his flock together. There is no doubt that his heart is in the right place. However, his influence brings no fundamental change in the minds and hearts of men.

It is Bimala, a woman facing the world for the first time, who shows the true meaning of patriotism. There is no question of self-interest in her when asked to sacrifice for the sake of the country and no task is too degrading for her. She is the zamindar's wife, a Chota Rani, a woman constantly trying to establish her superiority in the household over that of her widowed sister-in-law, the Bara Rani, very conscious of her high status, yet when she is asked to collect fifty thousand rupees, she says, "I will get it." She knows she will be found out, she knows she will be humiliated, but for the sake of the country no sacrifice is too great for her.

Initially dazzled by Sandip, Bimala becomes deeply committed to his brand of nationalism. However, when the hollowness of the movement is revealed to her, she swings back to the path of righteousness however politically and socially incorrect it may appear to be. Even at the risk of being exposed as a thief, she decides she would leave no stone unturned to save the immature Amulya. It is the same level of sacrifice and devotion that Tagore demanded from India's citizens in order to achieve true freedom.

Tagore believed that political and commercial aggressiveness was a Western concept. To achieve freedom and happiness, there was no need for India to imitate the Western political ideals of plunder and exploitation. The misguided pre-Gandhi nationalistic movement in India, Tagore believed, would make the poor people poorer and the political leaders would be the only gainers. True modernism lay in the freedom of the mind, not in slavery of tastes.

Unfortunately the blind following of Western ideas, totally foreign to the Indian psyche, had led to a growth of materialism. Base passions had been churned up. Thus men like Sandip, although not naturally evil, had become callous and selfish when they cynically harnessed the then current wave of nationalism.

Tagore believed that Indian society had too many weaknesses. The average Indian lacked sympathy for his fellow beings and the general inertia of its people was such as to make them easy tools in the hands of self-seeking politicians. Strengthening India's social fabric therefore, required the removal of age-old problems of caste and class. These problems, unique to India, were social and not political in nature.

India needed constructive work, uplifting of women and of the weaker sections of Indian society. India needed people who were ready to perform their duties in a spirit of self-sacrifice. The self-seeking politicians would merely create a huge organisation of slavery under the guise of freedom.

Bimala shows this way—renouncing the path of violence and terrorism she opts for harmonious development of man and unselfish love for her fellow human beings. There is no fear or doubt in her mind. Bimala, like Tagore, is convinced that this sense of morality and justice alone could ensure the freedom of the Indian nation. Otherwise by driving away the English, Indians would create a vacuum that could only attract other invaders to replace the British.

Critical Approaches to the Novel

The essays included in this anthology have been selected keeping in mind the needs of the graduate and research students of Rabindranath Tagore in general and of *The Home and the World* in particular. Some of the essays deal with the themes of *The Home and the World* while others focus more specifically on the individual characters, their inter-relationships and the concerns of Tagore.

While talking about the need to capture the "essence" of the original in the translated text also, Alpana Neogy discusses the contemporary relevance of the novel. The problems or "inadequacies" in the translated text are minimized if the translator has sufficient linguistic proficiency in both the languages and is well acquainted with the social, cultural, political and spiritual ethos that infuses the original text. A novel like Tagore's *Ghare Baire* or *The Home and the World* with its theme of swadeshi and "Nationalism" has prophetic overtones and depth. The arresting *atmakatha* style as part of the narrative strategy, makes it very suitable for translation into English in order to make it accessible to larger audiences in India and abroad, Neogy argues.

D.R. Shashidhara makes a detailed analysis of the questions relating to sexuality, feminism, identity of women, patriarchy, etc. in the context of the social environment rooted in tradition but getting exposed to winds of change in the beginning of the twentieth century when the freedom movement had started picking up some momentum. She traces the development of Tagore's insightful vision starting with *The Broken Nest* (1901) through *Two Sisters* (1933). The human aspect in the form of "marital relationships" is explored as an essential core in the structure of the plot of each one of these novels. The paper also offers a controversial angle on Tagore's philosophy of the Finite and the Infinite vis-à-vis his portrayal of man-woman relationship; and underscores a "paradox" behind Tagore's vision of the unifying Ideal and the fragmented Real.

In his presentation, Ranjan Ghosh explores Nikhil's character in great detail. By giving examples from the novel and quoting from Tagore's other works and works by Mahatma Gandhi, Aldous Huxley and others, he presents Nikhil as an introspective person who is in search of the real meaning of "nationalism," "swadeshi," "freedom," "fearlessness," etc. Nikhil experiments with truth in order to arrive at a harmonious vision of life. Through his eye, the thematic and narrative complexity of *The Home and the World* becomes self-evident to the reader. The much debated problem of "means and ends" which is still haunting India, emerges prophetically in this work.

Of the three main women characters in *The Home and the World*, Bimala, her widowed sister-in-law and Miss Gilby, it is Bimala's character that holds the reader's attention the most. Tagore closely analyses her character with reference to the question of "feminism" in a tradition-bound patriarchal society in pre-independence India. The backdrop of the swadeshi movement invests Bimala's character with a new dimension. Her role is that of a Goddess-Mother in conflict with her role as a Bimala of flesh and blood exposed to the wider world. Keya Majumdar presents an in-depth portrayal of this gifted Tagore heroine as visible through the aperture of a social kaleidoscope.

Can Tagore's novel be viewed as a socio-political and socio-cultural analytical treatise? Nandita Sinha's article answers this question in the affirmative with a portrayal of the multifaceted tumultuous world of the novel. She explores the multilayered theme of polarisation in the novel from the perspectives of conflicting individual relationships and disparate socio-political approaches.

Indira Bhatt attempts to follow the traumatic journey of the personae from illusion to self-awareness, and claims that Tagore's novels are more convincing as a psychological study than the works of his predecessors or contemporaries.

Vanashree Tripathy brings into focus another aspect of the novel relating particularly to its "Indianness" and the innate concept of *Dharma* as exemplified in the Hindu scriptures. She argues that the core issues raised in the novel belong to the wider realm of the Indian philosophical thought wherein the questions of human desires and sexuality are also given due importance. The interplay of human desires against the back-drop of socio-political forces unleashed by the swadeshi move-ment in the beginning of the twentieth century endow *The Home and the World* with a thematic complexity that one comes across only in very few novels.

Rahul Sapra's paper examines how Tagore analyses his views on "Nationalism" threadbare. Social, political, cultural and human dimensions, especially in the context of man-woman relationship, are portrayed with the help of three main characters in the novel. Tagore's prophetic vision/warning about the ugly face of "Nationalism" in the garb of aggres-sive and unethical politics are profound. His views remain relevant even today. Sapra also brings out the novelist's em-phasis on the need of emergence of a global order based on spiritual ethics interfaced with human needs and desires.

Basavraj Naikar analyzes the novel from the perspective of its main theme, i.e. the quest for liberation from foreign rule as symbolised through the swadeshi movement and boycott of foreign goods. Though the movement is apparently nationalis-tic, it creates its own set of economic, financial, social and communal problems. Bimala, the central character of *The Home and the World*, becomes the victim of these paradoxical situations and with the help of the characters of Sandip, an unscrupulous pragmatist, and Nikhil, a self-effacing rationalist, Tagore examines, along with the soico-political theme, the en-igmatic theme of man-woman relationship at the emotional level. Naikar also stresses the need for a shift and reorientation of Eurocentric theoretical approach in studying a typically Tagorean novel, as appropriately advocated by Anita Desai as well.

Tagore poses a number of queries in the novel about the background and justification of the swadeshi movement and the nature of reality and freedom. The article by Novy Kapadia shows that swadeshi was not an all-embracing struggle involving the lower classes and castes and all religions but an urban movement imposed on poor traders and peasants. Tagore's views on the dangers of a jingoism are shown as similar to the ideas expressed by noted Marxist scholar Randhir Singh on how nationalism serves as both a liberationist force and the means of domination. The essay also illustrates similarities between Tagore's views on ideological nationalism and those of Aijaz Ahmed expressed in *A Century of Revolution*.

The novel, in Pradip Lahiri's opinion, has a great socio-moral significance. Bimala in *The Home and the World* submitted to no coercion of any sort, but to a moral and perhaps spiritual ideology. Even in a rich and adequately comfortable household, a woman like Bimala started finding it hard not to feel frustrated, and not to suffer from an acute sense of non-fulfilment. Her idolized husband, more often than not, failed to come up to complement this sense of isolation in her reflective midriff, owing to their ordinary or cowardly over-inflated or arrogant, pretentious or indifferent, bland or dumb nature. A sense of stifled existential agony was almost imperceptibly surfacing.

A large body of critical response to Tagore's *The Home and the World* focuses on the woman question (especially in relation to Bimala and her encounter with the world beyond the threshold), tradition and modernity, materialism and spirituality and moral values, and the theme of nationalism and patriotism. Not much attention has been paid to the influence of Gandhi on Tagore's thinking even though the two were contemporaries and were in touch with each other. Subhash Chandra examines the concept of swadeshi in *The Home and the World* in the light of Gandhian thought, particularly his ideas contained in the *Hind Swaraj*.

Teaching Translated Literature: A Study of *The Home and the World*

ALPANA NEOGY

It is a scientific fact that no two persons ever see the same rainbow. According to the laws of physics, each observer sees sunlight refracted by a unique set of raindrops that produces a private rainbow, one for each observer. Technically, therefore, no two rainbows are exactly the same. Yet, this slight difference in each point of view does not prevent a rainbow to be as colourful and sublime as any other rainbow. Similarly, provided that a gifted translator translates a great work of literature, the translation too, becomes a work of art in spite of small differences.

I concede that the translation of any literary text—regional or national—will lead to some degradation of the original text. It is impossible to convey the linguistic, cultural and social nuances peculiar to any region or nation in another language.

To prove my point, in the Bengali text of *Ghare Baire*, Rabindranath Tagore begins with Bimala's *atmakatha*: "Ma go."[1] Surendranath Tagore in *The Home and the World* translates this as "Mother"[2] when perhaps "Mother dear" would have been more appropriate. Surendranath goes on to talk of the "vermilion mark at the parting" of the mother's hair and the wide red border "sari" (17) she wore. He thoughtfully provides us with notes telling us that the vermilion mark is the mark of "Hindu wifehood" and that the sari is the "dress of the Hindu woman." (17) The sentence concludes with the mother's "wonderful eyes" being "full of depth and peace."

(17) In the Bengali text, Rabindranath Tagore says, "shayee tomaar duti chokh [they are not 'wonderful']—shanto, snigdho, gobheer." (5)

The purists may proclaim that the translation is flawed as Surendranath had not provided an apt translation for "snigdho" (loving) but had used appropriate adjectives for "shanto" and "gobheer."

Why then translate and what is the purpose of teaching translated literature? Translations convey to people speaking in a different language, the essence of a text that possesses universal appeal. There is no doubt that the quality of any translation depends a great deal on the knowledge and capability of the translator in both the concerned languages.

Surendranath Tagore, Gurudev's nephew, was assigned the task of translating *Ghare Baire* and the Penguin edition of *The Home and the World* was used in the teaching of the text to the students of B.A. (English Honours) First Year at Delhi University. Surendranath must have been considered most appropriate for the job for he had spent his formative years in England and was, therefore, fluent in both English and Bengali. He must have interacted with his illustrious uncle while translating the novel and the manuscript was sent for publication to Macmillan in Great Britain in 1919 only after Rabindranath Tagore had given to it his stamp of approval.

E.M. Forster, we are told, deplored the translation's language for its "Babu sentences" and for the "boarding-house flirtation that masks itself in patriotic talk."[3] Georg Lukacs, too, had condemned the translation as "a petit bourgeois yarn of the shoddiest kind."[4] According to Anita Desai, "such criticism has to be taken into account because it was levelled at the winner of the Nobel Prize for Literature and because Tagore had often been compared to Tolstoy." (71)

So, with all the "babu sentences," my students, all Indians, no Bengalis, many of them adept at babu sentences themselves, and I attempted to understand the novel! I firmly believe that never did we feel that we were not being able to grasp the true essence of Tagore because the text was a translated one. Perhaps the students found the long discussions between Sandip and Nikhil tiresome. But such long passages exist in the original Bengali text as well. They also exist in many other texts prescribed for study. In Charlotte Bronte's *Jane Eyre*, for example,

On the other hand, even though this novel had been written in the early 20th century, my students found it astonishingly relevant and interesting even at the end of that century. Nirad C. Chaudhuri believed that the tragedy of India lay in the fact that "with rare exceptions political activity and agitation became the business of an insufficiently educated, insufficiently intelligent, insufficiently cultured, though serious and earnest minded class and this gradually brought down the standard of political life till it seemed to have become the monopoly of pig-headed fools and faddists."[5]

Tagore's novel, though not in such colourful a language, virtually had a similar story to tell. In Sandip we found the archetype of the modern day politician who does not have any scruples while he furthers his own interests. The mindless riots, the strikes, the terrorism so real in the novel appear real to us, too. To that extent, the novel could well have been a contemporary story! We could only marvel at the perspicacity of the writer—how well he had understood the Indian psyche! Bimala is not the only one to be carried away by Sandip's rhetoric and hypocrisy. The austere Nikhils of this world are considered to be too relentless and inflexible. They have few followers. It is the Sandips who hold sway with their swashbuckling ways and their swagger.

At the 50th anniversary of the Indian Republic, President K.R. Narayanan spoke of providing a "safe pedestrian crossing" for the unempowered as India sped on "the three way fast lane of liberalisation, globalisation and privatisation."[6] The economic reforms must reach the poor, he said. Tagore had virtually said the same thing when he opposed the Swadeshi movement and felt that the movement had gone out of control and had turned violent. The elite class, he felt, was exploiting the misdirected youth and the unlettered labourer. At that moment of time, Tagore was considered a betrayer, someone who had sold his soul to the West!

We also considered the novel as a psychological novel as we tried to understand the three main characters. Bimala is a typical Indian girl trying to come out of her sequestered existence at the beginning of the century. She has hardly interacted with anyone outside the confines of her home. We understand and sympathise with her when she is attracted to the crafty and manipulative Sandip, her husband's friend. He flatters her and makes her believe that she is the Shakti, the force behind the Swadeshi movement. We watch helplessly as she steals the family jewels for this movement. We do not condemn her for her actions but empathise with her emotions. She has not seen enough of the world and it is but natural for her to believe the wily Sandip. By writing this novel through *atmakathas* or diaries of the three figures, Tagore is able to illustrate the female psyche just as he has understood the two diametrically opposite male characters, Sandip and Nikhil.

My plea is, look at the whole book in its entirety. Has the book managed to convey the essence of the original text? Is the characterisation as near as possible to the original? Is the emphasis, home and the home background, the political and social milieu at the beginning of the twentieth century, similar to the original? If it is, which it is, let us not bemoan the fact that certain paragraphs have been omitted in the translated text. These omissions do not in any way detract from the merit of the translated text.

Any good literature, no matter in which language it may be written, retains its essence when it is translated well. If the subject of a text has universal appeal and if the art and craft of the author is of a high order, something very worthwhile will be retained after the translation which will continue to delight readers brought up in other tongues.

The purpose of translated literary texts is not to convey exactitude, as this is impossible. In the applied fields of medicine or science, the chemical composition of a medicine, for example, or of the exact procedure of building a rocket does not permit even the slightest deviation from the original text.

However, in the case of literary texts, one does not deal with procedures and objects. Instead one deals with thoughts, emotions, beliefs and ideas. Hence the need for exactitude is not of the essence. In translated literature, the endeavour is to capture the core, the sweep and the panorama. Therefore, if we seek exactitude for its own sake while evaluating translations of great works, we risk losing focus of the underlying theme. In our preoccupation with individual trees, we risk losing sight of the majestic sweep of the woods.

NOTES

1. (Calcutta: Vishwabharati Granthanvibhag, 1994), p. 5.
2. Rabindranath Tagore, *The Home and the World*, trans. Surendranath Tagore (London: Penguin Books, 1985), p. 17.
3. Introduction by Anita Desai
4. *Loc. cit.*
5. Nirad C. Chaudhuri, *A Passage to England* (Macmillan, 1959), p. 192.
6. *Times of India*, January 26, 2000, p. 1.

Social Dynamics of the Oedipus Complex in Tagore's Fiction

D.R. SHASHIDHARA

Tagore's preoccupation with the Oedipal juxtapositions in terms of the mother-mistress dichotomy can be seen in his very first novel *Binodini*. Introducing Mahendra, the protagonist of the novel, Tagore tells us:

> Eating or resting, at work or at leisure, he needed his mother to hover round him. Like a Kangaroo cub he continued to nestle in the maternal pouch long after he had been released from the womb. (1)

This Kangaroo cub "loves his mother more than sons normally do." That is why his mother Rajalakshmi is said to have been accused of deliberately not letting him marry for the fear of losing him to the bride. The accusation proves to be too true. Once Mahendra marries Ashalata, the mother sycophant transfers all his attention and loyalty to his new wife. Thus the bride, as feared, ousts the mother.

But more than such fictional representation of the Oedipal situation, what interests me is the socio-political overtones these situations acquire in Tagore's later novels. Since these nuances seem to be deeply entrenched in the nineteenth century reform movements concerning women's emancipation and the definition of an Indian identity, a brief appraisal of these socio-political pressures becomes necessary.

Sumit Sarkar remarks in his *A Critique of Colonial India*, "women's emancipation came to occupy an absolutely central position in the concerns of the nineteenth century intelligentsia." (71) It happened so because of "certain acute problems of inter-personal adjustments." (73) Referring, rather curiously, to Rabindranath Tagore's poem *Nabadampatir Premaalap*, he says, "Rabindranath's hilarious poem about spouting romantic verse before a wife still engrossed with her dolls reflected a very serious problem." (73) These very real and serious problems were problems of inter-personal adjustments within a family and they were sought to be eased out by educating women. The dual purpose of emancipating wives and imposing upon them certain "puritanical restraints" was sought to be achieved by doing so. Charges of 'licentiousness' levelled against the Brahmo movement and Brahmo households necessitated it. Quoting Kate Millett's *Sexual Politics*, he notes that this prudishness insisted on the relinquishment of sexuality and demanded sexual inhibition in a woman if she were to maintain her social status. While Sumit Sarkar's conjectures could be quite right, they do not wholly explain the ideological need to create an asexual modern woman. It is precisely here that Partha Chatterjee's readings in Nationalist ideologies and the definition of an Indian identity prove invaluable.

Partha Chatterjee argues that nationalism provided an answer to the problems concerning the position of woman in a modern society in terms of its own ideological paradigms. The ideological paradigm was defined "by a separation of the domain of culture into two spheres—the material and the spiritual." (237) The material/spiritual distinction further yielded an "analogous but ideologically far more powerful dichotomy: that between the outer and the inner." (238) He explains that when we apply the inner/outer distinction to the concrete realities of day-to-day life, we

> get a separation of the social space in *ghar* and *bahir*, the home and the world. The world is the external, the domain of the material, the home represents our inner spiritual self, our true identity. It is typically the domain of the male. The home in its essence must remain unaffected by the profane activities of the material world and

> woman is its representation. And so we get an identification of social roles by gender to correspond with the separation of the social space into ghar and bahir. (238-39)

The burden of sustaining the inner spirituality of indigenous social life implied that "There would have to be a marked *difference* in the degree and manner of westernization of women, as distinct from men, in the modern world of the nation." (243) The role that education played in preparing the women to shoulder the burden is thus expressed:

> Education was meant to inculcate in women the virtues—the typically 'bourgeois' virtues characteristic of the new social forms of 'disciplining—of orderliness, thrift, cleanliness and a personal sense of responsibility, the practical skills of literacy, accounting and hygiene and the ability to run the household according to the new physical and economic conditions set by the outside world. For this, she would also need to have some idea of the world outside the home in which she could even venture as long as it did not threaten her 'femininity.' It is this later criterion, now invested with a characteristically nationalist content, which made possible the displacement of the boundaries of 'the home' from the physical confines earlier defined by the rules of purdah (seclusion) to a more flexible, but culturally nonetheless determinate, domain. (247)

The relevance of these definitions to Tagore's fiction can be made clear with the following quotation:

> This patriarchy combined coercive authority with the subtle force of persuasion. This was expressed most generally in an inverted ideological form of the relation of power between the sexes: the adulation of woman as goddess or as mother. Whatever be its sources in the classical religions of India or in medieval religious prac-

> tices, it is undeniable that the specific ideological form in which we know the Sati-Savitri-Sita construct in the modern literature and arts of India today is wholly a product of the development of a dominant middle class culture coeval with the era of nationalism. It served to emphasize with all the force of mythological inspiration what had in any case become a dominant characteristic of femininity in the new woman, viz. the 'spiritual' qualities of self-sacrifice, benevolence, devotion, religiosity, etc. (248-49)

At this stage a reference to the fictional transformations such ideologies undergo could be crucial in the eventual comprehension of the implications of these ideologies in terms of the inter-personal relationships within the marital context.

The exercise could be conveniently begun with a reference to Tagore's first novel *Broken Nest*. It is here that we first see the havoc the prevalent ideological condition played in the domestic world of inter-personal relationships. The novella concerns Bhupati's (a very significant name, as indeed most of the proper nouns in Tagore are) preoccupations with the outer world and its consequences. His tryst with the external world gets represented in his journalistic ventures. Tagore describes the immediate and implied consequence of such a venture in the following manner:

> While he was hypnotized by the newspaper, his girl-wife Charulatha gradually stepped into young womanhood. The newspaper editor did not take sufficient note of this noteworthy event. His attention was fixed on the government's border policy, which was running wild. (26)

The inattention thus begun runs its logical course till it results in an unbridgeable gap between Bhupati and his wife Charulata. But the colonial external world, which is by definition filled to its brim with treachery, duplicity, selfishness and moral unscruple leaves him a bankrupt. Then,

> His body pricked with terror when he saw that aspect of world which had just been unmasked. Like a frightened man who in the face of a flash flood, looks for the highest ground and runs towards it, Bhupati went swiftly from the fear-ridden outer world to the inner rooms of his own house. He said to himself whatever else happens, Charu won't deceive me. (72)

But he is tragically mistaken.

> He seemed to share the common belief that no one need earn his claim to his wife—the wife keeps her own lamp burning like the polestar. It is not blown out by the wind. It need not be filled with oil. When the outside of Bhupati's home began to crack, it did not even occur to him to examine cracks of the arches of the inner of rooms. (83)

But Bhupati's tragedy, when compared with those of his later brethren seems mild, for he is only left in darkness. After all, this rejector of the wife and domestic world is not accosted by the 'mistress.'

For the mistress to accost the men of the world, the 'wife' will have to possess a more precisely defined identity. The definition in fact, occurs in *Gora* during a hot argument between Gora and Binoy regarding the real identity of woman. The debate which occurs after Binoy meets Sucharita, a young Brahmo girl living with Paresh Babu, is as follows:

> 'The scriptures tell us,' persisted Gora, 'that woman is deserving of worship because she gives light to the home—the honour which is given by English custom, because she sets fire to the hearts of men, had better not be termed worship.'
>
> 'Would you contemptuously dismiss a great idea because it occasionally gets clouded over?' asked Binoy.
>
> 'Binu,' answered Gora impatiently, 'I affirm that all the exaggerated language about woman that you find in

> English books has at bottom merely desire. The altar at which woman may be truly worshipped is her place as Mother, the seat of the pure, right minded Lady of the House. . . . The cause of your mind hovering about Paresh Babu's house, like a mother round a candle, is in plain language what the English call 'Love'; but for God's sake, don't ape the English culture by lacing this love above all other considerations, as the one object of man's worship.' (9)

Thus the debate, while making clear its preference for the 'Mother' identity, sets the 'Lover' against it. In fact, as we shall presently see, almost all Tagore's heroes end up in getting caught in this Mother/Lover (mistress) dichotomy. It is interesting at this stage to note that the ideologically preferred identity of the Mother is not one that a woman is born with and it is the gaining of this identity that characterizes the growth of all the heroines of Tagore. The acquisition itself is quite an arduous task beset with fatal traps for all of them. The orphan girl Kamala, in *The Wreck*, has to witness and withstand the natural fury of a storm while on board a boat to discover her 'Lady of the House' identity. Ramesh, who is unaware of Kamala's trial by the storm is struck by the overnight transformation, when he sees her on the next day:

> It was evident that Kamala had taken sole command and assumed the entire responsibility. . . . The face in which she had meekly accepted Ramesh's dictates had come to an abrupt close. (173)

But within the framework of *The Wreck* itself, this is Kamala's first step towards her identity. She has to pass through many an ordeal before she can enter her home as the accomplished 'Lady of the House.' Ashalata's growth, though described in similar terms, differs from Kamala's in that it has to pass the litmus test of sexuality. The sexual indulgence of Mahendra and Ashalata destroys Mahendra's home in more ways than one. Asha can discover her identity and take charge of the house only after a considerable period of sexual abstinence. As this idea of the transcendence of sexuality gets woven into the very fabric of *The Home and the World*, Ashalata need not hold our attention anymore. It needs only to be remarked that 'this slip of a girl,' an 'inept wife' 'schooled by suffering' gets transformed to hold "the reins of the household in her hands" (220) by the end of the novel.

It was suggested earlier that the identity of the mother is not an inherited one, but one that is earned by hard labour. But, Bimala, the heroine of *The Home and the World*, is more fortunate. 'Fortunate' because she not only has auspicious birth marks and signs but also resembles her mother, an epitome of Indian womanhood. But even for such a fortunate woman as Bimala, the maternal identity does not come easily:

> Had I not stepped into my good fortune by a mere chance, and without deserving it? . . . God may grant us gifts but the merit of being able to take and hold them must be our own. (15)

The storm that she has to weather is not just a natural phenomenon, but the very tempest of Nationalism that gets coupled with passionate sex. In fact she has to pass through the phase of a mistress:

> possibly this is woman's nature, when her passion is roused, she poses all her sensibility for all that is outside it. When, like the river, we women keep to our banks, we give nourishment with all that we have. When we overflow them we destroy with all that we are. (59)

How eventually this childless wife secures her maternal identity in the context of extramarital temptations and the nationalist upsurge and to what extent and in what manner are her quests doctored are besides the point. What should immediately concern us is the fact that Nikhil, like the other knights of the world, is tied to Bimala.

Tagorean knight errants of the world, though bound to the

chosen mother figure, are in the constant company of the westernized, modernized beloveds who are freely available. The beloved may be, as it happens with Mahendra, a widow like the westernized Binodini, who is unlike Ashalata, an expert in the art of love or she could be one's own unmarried sister-in-law as it happens with Shashanka of *Two Sisters*. Shashanka is a dedicated servant of the world. A contractor by profession, he is committed to his work. This is what Tagore says about Shashanka's relationships with work: "Unbending was this work, which cared for none, which ignored everything—the wife's entreaties, the invitations to friends, his own comfort even." (24) But his wife Sharmila, as Tagore tells us, is of the mother-kind. Her features and attire suggest "homely grace rather than elegance of style." (1) But her sister Urmila, belongs to the "beloved kind." This is one of her descriptions:

> She dressed simply but elegantly; knew how to bring out the full beauty of the figure in a sari by a slight turn here, a right twist there—in a way whose secret no one could catch. (35)

This 'mysterious, enchanting beloved, unlike the wife who was barred from having any access to the man's world, can even assist them there as well. Therefore, Shashanka is tempted by Urmila to step out of his marital relationship. But Tagore's providential hand saves his marriage. But the temptation, as it generally happens, ends in Shashanka's bankruptcy.

For Nikhil, the 'mistress' presents herself as his 'Eternal Love.' He tells us that his endeavour in his marital life was to discover her in his wife Bimala. He declares his absolute faith in her when he says, "No, my Eternal Love cannot deceive me, for she is true!" (81) His attempts to realize her in Bimala include the appointment of an English tutor, Miss Gilby to modernize her. But when Bimala prefers Sandip to him, this is what he says:

> I think I have come to the verge of understanding one

> thing. Man has so fanned the flame of the loves of men and women, as to make over pass its rightful domain, and now, even in the name of humanity itself, he cannot bring it back under control. Man's worship has idolized his passion. (110)

That is, he has not heeded to Gora's caution. The mother-mistress dichotomy tragi-ironically tears him away from his home and wife:

> We men are Knights whose quest is that freedom to which our ideals cause us. She who makes for us the banner under which we fare forth is the true woman for us. We must tear away the disguise of her who weaves our net of enchantment at home, and know for what she is. We must beware of clothing her in the witchery of our longings and imaginings and thus allow her to distract us from our quest. (143-44)

That is back to square one. Perhaps it is not just that. For, as Nikhil himself puts it, men like him, "In trying to manufacture a helpmate . . . spoil a wife." (272) This, then, is the penalty exacted by the definition of an Indian identity presented in terms of a nationalist paradigm derived of several severe oppositions. Perhaps this is the place where we should consider the open endings of these novels. All these novels centred around a marital relationship end in a tense hope as in *Broken Nest* and *The Home and the World* or with a promise of the possibility of future reconciliation and happiness, as in the case of *Binodini*, *The Wreck* and *Two Sisters*. In the light of the foregoing discussion while the tense hope seems to be suggestive of an ideological dead end, the promise of a future happiness looks shallow.

A discussion of any of Tagore's canonical work is incomplete if it fails to bring within its ambit his preferred ideology of the relations of the Infinite and Finite aspects of reality. Tagore's attempts to define these marital relations in terms of the infinite's paradoxical relationships with the finite was equally doomed to failure as Nikhil's failure to yoke the opposites together. But what can indeed be suggested at the end is the possible ideological motives behind Tagore's paradoxical ideals: a fragmented world compellingly demanding a unifying ideology.

Works Cited

Chatterjee, Partha. "The Nationalist Resolution of Women's Question" in *Recasting Women*, ed. Sangari and Vaid. New Delhi: Kali for Women.

Sarkar, Sumit. *A Critique of Colonial India*. Calcutta: Papyrus, 1985.

Tagore, Rabindranath. *The Broken Nest*, trans. Mary M. Lago & Supuria Bari, *Nashtanir* (1901). Macmillan India, 1985.

______. *Binodini*, trans. Krishna Kripalani from *Chokher Bali* (1903). New Delhi, Sahitya Akademi, 1959.

______. *The Wreck*, trans. J.G. Drummond, from *Nauka Dubi* (1906). New Delhi: Macmillan, rpt. 1985.

______. *Gora*, trans. W.W. Pearson from *Gora* (1910). Macmillan, 1985.

______. *The Home and the World*, trans. Surendranath Tagore from *Ghare-Baire* (1916). Macmillan, 1985.

______. *Two Sisters*, trans. Krishna Kripalani from *Dui Bon* (1933). Calcutta: Vishwa Bharati, 1986.

Experiments with Truth and Nikhil's Quest for a Harmonic Vision

RANJAN GHOSH

Every quest of man begins with the worm of conflict turning within him. More often it is a tension that springs from a search for a security in this fragile world and the yearning for something in him which is superior to nature. Among the major characters in *The Home and the World*, Nikhil emerges as the one with a strong positive inner tension that goads him to conduct various experiments with truth. Truth is explored at various levels in the novel and experiments lead to a realization that refuses to be partisan on any issues. For me, Nikhil is the epitome of Truth that has a classical character with the principles of balance and restraint working under a ceaseless self-introspection. It is a Truth which is not impervious to reason and judgment and runs counter to Sandip's Truth—the flaming ebullient expression of an indomitable energy. It matures with 'open spaces' which are put under the steady glow of an unabated soul-searching. His relation with Bimala is a self-scrutiny for his wife stands as a meaningful 'vacillation' which is entombed in a restlessness that comes from the competing claims of a classical restraint (Nikhil, interpreted as sedate and bland) and a romantic exuberance (Sandip, interpreted as a charismatic effervescence). Nikhil's truth realizes the inability in Bimala to blossom fully in her power under his calm ministration. He realizes as well the necessity to relinquish some claims grounded in conventional rights if one is to find a person fully revealed in truth. His truth is never dogmatic; rather his pragmatics allow him to test the strength and vulnerability of it with the touchstone of his inner being and greater being of the world and the cosmos. It is a truth that allows all the rays of inspection to fall on it. Bimala chooses to be disenchanted for it enshrines patience, lacks turbulence and refuses to be unjust. Sandip's truth proved magnetic as he charmed his way into Bimala's heart through rhetorical glamour and conspicuous boisterousness, commanding a respect that is built partially on fear. Nikhil's truth refuses to succumb despite the reality of its present dilemma and the 'grounds' he has to forfeit.

> I hoped that when Bimala found herself free in the outer world she would be rescued from her infatuation for tyranny. But now I feel sure that this infatuation is deep down in her nature. Her love is for the boisterous. From the tip of her tongue to the pit of her stomach she must tingle with red pepper in order to enjoy the simple fare of life. But my determination was, never to do my duty with frantic impetuosity, helped on by the fiery liquor of excitement. I know Bimala finds it difficult to respect me for this, taking my scruples for feebleness,—and she is quite angry with me because I am not running amuck crying *Bande Mataram.*[1]

Here, the three words—'infatuation,' 'impetuosity' and 'determination'—hold a key to Nikhil's growth to a Harmony. Despite the arrowheads of criticism, Nikhil stamps a determination to harness the profound inner power of man, which is never amorphous. In his growth to a vision, he recognizes infatuation or franticness as a mere bubble that cannot pour a clean clear drop into the river of life; the fatuity and fragility of it forestall the environment to merge in the ultimate 'sea.' It is a stutter in the road to realize the Energy in us, the Energy that can

> Shake me out of this cringing in the dust,
> Out of the fetters that shackle our mind,
> make futile our destiny;
> Out of the unreason that bends our

dignity down under the indiscriminate
feet of dictators;
Shatter this age-long shame of ours,
And raise our head
into the boundless sky,
into the generous light,
into the air of freedom. "Boundless Sky"

Indeed Nikhil's truth has unshackled itself from the fetters of depressing conventions and meretriciousness of catchy shibboleths. It develops into an aura of authority that does not require the external stimulus to energize it. Truth is energy itself; it has a vitality quite opposed to any impulsiveness that goads us to go berserk to prove a point of our existence. It is synonymous with self-government analogous to an Emersonian self-reliance. To Emerson, as to Nikhil, nothing is more sacred than the integrity of one's mind and no law other than that of one's own nature can be considered sacred. Nikhil's truth has a 'non conformity' that is never deleterious but is enduring and enlightening. His truth is whipped with the displeasure of the world but its ring of inviolability knows that moronic consistency is the 'hobgoblin of little minds.' So

> Trust thyself: every heart vibrates to that iron string. Accept the place the divine providence has found for you, the society of your contemporaries, the connection of events.[2]

In fact the question that troubles such a truth is whether it lacks imagination. Imagination fuelled by infatuation and frantic impetuosity cannot conjugate with the Harmony of man's home and the world. Imagination needs to light the lamp that has enough oil to burn. It can then lead to a clear vision of the home-world phenomenon. Here imagination has the truth of creation that suspires from the essence of virtue and wakes up to exercise judgment. It is in conflict with the principle of excess (not Tagore's principle of surplus) and sanctifies a place beyond the hard premises of factual reality. Here imagination provides the 'value' that is never trampled by fact. Contrary to Sandip's charge that he lacks imagination, Nikhil exhibits an imaginative power that throws him creatively into the world without evading the home-truths. It removes the scales from his eyes, shakes hands with the 'possible' and crosses swords with exaggeration. It is a vision that takes account of the perils of the foamy sea before mounting the waves. It is the inspiration without the intransigent impulse that prepares the garden with the flowers of reason, prescience and sanity. Imagination for Nikhil bespeaks of a future that takes adequate measure of the present, it enlightens him to understand the 'freedom from and freedom to' dynamics. His imagination is the blessed vision of the Socratic Chandranathbabu that has taught him to have faith in faith and *wait* with the freedom of mind that never flusters in course of a stormy passage from the narrow to the larger world. It is the imagination that has taught him how Force loses all its force before Truth.

II

In the quest for Harmony, Nikhil's Truth readily understands the futility of nursing any extravagant hope and indeed believes in the Grecian principle of restraint. His truth negates the truth of Sandip that deifies Bimala. On the contrary, Bimala is what she is. It is preposterous to expect that she should assume the role of an angel for his pleasure. He understands that despite his avidity for imaginary perfection, the Creator is under no obligation to supply him with angels.

Nikhil, to my mind, is Greek in a way. He weds thought with morality and wisdom with virtue. His imagination precludes the bane of preconception. The force of human truth makes him vibrate with human energies. He manifests a truthful seeing of the world and recognizes the balance our life maintains. It echoes mildly, though meaningfully, Pindar in Nemean, viii, 32.

> Some pray for gold, and some for vast lands; but I to please my countrymen, and so to hide my limbs beneath

> the earth, praising where praise is due, and sowing blame for sinful men. Virtue grows and blooms, like a tree that shoots up under fostering dews, when skilled men and dust raise it towards the liquid air. . . . Among my fellow-citizens I look with brightness in my eye, not having overstepped due bounds, and having removed from before my feet all violence. My future time come kindly to me.[3]

Indeed nothing that is good and fulfilling is lost; the music stops, sometimes, it must. But the goodness of the ineffable something which moves one while it lasts, cannot become a nothingness. It is the harmony of Everlasting Love that demands the perceiver to break through the surface shrubbery of sordid materialism. Nikhil's truth encompasses the 'image' in all its disparate experiences. It is the image that Nikhil cannot wield his authority over; it is to which his vision of truth leads him. The more Nikhil approximates his Love, the more he is unshackled from self-deception. "The unveiled star tells me not to fear. That which is eternal must always be there." (81) Indeed there is a stinging irony in the lament:

> It is August, the sky breaks into a passionate rain;
> Alas, empty is my house. (108)

Nikhil feels the emptiness for a while because he has not yet realized the warmth of Harmony which soothes him in the end. What stands disqualified, I believe, is the statement: "My house, I now see, was built to remain empty, because its doors cannot open." (109) It cannot open because it cannot lubricate under the truth of Sandip's belligerence and Bimala's precarious moral oscillation. Emptiness in marital life can inevitably come when life understands the monopolist formula to celebrate a perennial union among the blossoming water-lilies. Unfortunately, it ignores the other octave of life. Self can at times become an incarceration that refuses to grant freedom. Freedom from untruth can come from a certain 'detachment' from the lesser course of life. Nikhil looks at the flowers in withered black scattered round his portrait and avers: "Never mind; let me welcome truth, albeit in such sere and sorry garb, and look forward to the time when I shall be able to do so unmoved, as does my photograph." (111) There is an 'attachment' to the greater course that never overpasses its rightful domain and forbids future to congeal into one solid mass settling on his breast. "The great world stretches far beyond, and one can truly measure one's joys and sorrows when standing in its midst." (113)

There is a snag in Nikhil's apprehension of harmony in the sense that he has misconstrued the balance between particularity and generality to an extent. Actuality and Ideality (in the Platonian sense) demands a complementary tension: "When the actualities of everyday things get the better of the man, then is Truth lost sight of and freedom missed." (115) And it is from this sore point of imbalance that emptiness spins its web around. Man tinkers with Harmony when he fails to forsake the desire to 'magnify' and superimposes his premeditation in the conjuring of an image of the world (Sandip's predicament). The contrariety in the luxury of the passionate rain that overwhelms the sky and the 'emptiness' that plagues the heart holds implicitly the passport to the gates of Harmony. Nikhil's experiments with truths educate him to accept the duality—the thesis and antithesis of life. One can here meaningfully point to Nikhil's realization to view Bimala's adornment as a thing apart from herself—the dialectic between Truth as it exists and Truth with ornate appurtenances. The march to the Harmony can teach the importance of breaking barriers and the efficacy of building them as well. Nikhil's Truth triumphs in this game of construction and destruction to realize the individual reality of 'emptiness' and the 'passionate rain.' The synthesis makes him Lao Tzu's 'sound man' who by not advancing himself stays further ahead of himself, refusing to confine himself to himself sustains himself outside himself and being never an end in himself he endlessly becomes himself.

Therefore a sound man shalt so square the circle
And circle the square as not to injure not to impede:

The glow of his life shall not daze,
It shall lead.[4]

III

A Gandhi-like Nikhil asserts with confidence: "It is my feelings that are outraged, whenever you try to pass off injustice as a duty, and unrighteousness as a moral idea. The fact, that I am incapable of stealing, is not due to my possessing logical faculties, but to my having some feeling of respect for myself and love for ideals." (38) In fact his metapolitics is people-oriented where it is important to know the country in frank reality. His truth openly refuses to make use of hypnotic texts of patriotism. The aggressive nationalism that raises the nation to the status of a demi-god is perilous. Nikhil, here, is voicing Tagore's political ideas that believed in respecting not just the ideals of one's own people but the ideals and traditions of other people as well. A blind worship of the Nation state holds dark portents for the human civilisation as two ghastly world wars have revealed. Nikhil's political vision is permeated by the religion of restraint and tolerance that concentrates on the need to serve humanity. Nikhil finds truth in the plurality of religious traditions for he believes that there cannot be a true and perfect religion.

> "We can be staunch in our convictions," I said, "but we have no control over those of others. For all that many of us are Vaishnavas, those of us who are Shaktas go on with their animal sacrifices just the same. That cannot be helped. We must, in the same way, let the Mussulmans do as they think best. So please refrain from all disturbance." (218)

So the truth of politics need not be sought with the help of illusions; his truth rebuffs the principle of imperious dominance in religion and politics and indeed if religion has to permeate into politics he prescribes an aversion to worship 'false gods.' Giving wide berth to 'drunkenness' in patriotism, he emphasises the need for self-government as self-governance leads to self-respect. "He rules himself in such a manner that he is never a hindrance to his neighbour."[5]

Swaraj, for Nikhil, is the freedom that never usurps the right of any community but ensures even-handed justice and fair treatment to all. Gandhi-like, he points out, "If the idea of a United India is a true one," objects Nikhil, "Mussalmans are a necessary part of it." (158) Nikhil's Truth, like Gandhi, professes an affirmation of the unity of mankind and realizes the identity of the real self in his desire to live in a united non-violent world. The Truth proposes action that is taken in accordance with the merit of circumstances and considers aggression preferable to cowardice. Nikhil's statement—"But I must refuse to tyrannize"—cannot be stigmatized with cowardice. "Cowardice and Ahimsa do not go together any more than water and fire."[6] Nikhil's refusal to tyrannize despite having the power to wield is far from cravenness for it demands discipline and intrepidity. He journeys to the unity of his selves by a fearlessness and love that rejoices in the essential unity of all life. This is satyagraha for Nikhil.

> "Our country," I tried to explain, "has been brought to death's door through sheer fear,—from fear of the gods down to fear of the police; and if you set up, in the name of the freedom, the fear of some other bogey, whatever it may be called; if you raise your victorious standard on the cowardice of the country by means of downright oppression, then no true lover of the country can bow to your decision." (171)

In fact, this living sentiment of ahimsa, is not meekness. It is one of the potent means for him to reach the harmony of existence: "This meekness is not submission, or mere passive endurance of wrong or injustice: such submission would be cowardly and would imply co-operation, even though involuntary, with the power of tyranny."[7]

In this perpetual challenge to the insolence of the strong lies Nikhil's authority and integrity of *dharma*. Gandhi-like he never chooses to coerce anyone into believing his principles. One's moral dilemmas need not cast a shadow on others; one's belief in the definition of duty need not transgress the realm of duty of others. So, to a large extent, Nikhil's Truth is synonymous with non-violence. Like Gandhi, he glorifies individual liberty which is perhaps a pointer to enlightened anarchy and the definition that Gandhi reserves for the Vedic term *Swaraj*. (It may be worthwhile for us to note that Tagore disagreed with Gandhi on several scores of the non co-operation movement especially on the burning of the foreign clothes. In my estimate, most often, Nikhil is the Tagorean Gandhi.) Nikhil's truth reveals the necessity to understand the term where individual rights are not infringed or menacingly overridden and no moral coercion is entertained. "But if fear is to regulate how people are to dress, where they shall trade, or what they must eat, then is man's freedom of will utterly ignored, and manhood destroyed at the root." (172)

Nikhil's Truth has learnt with self experiments the futility to live up to an 'image.' Truth resides in embracing our original nature which like the river spreads its warmth and life on either side of the bank without the hint of harm. Nikhil revolts against Bimala's suggestion that if tyranny is unleashed for the sake of the country it ceases to be blatant tyranny. With a rare aplomb, he retorts: "To tyrannise for the country is to tyrannise over the country. But that I am afraid you will never understand." (142) This goes to show that the harmony towards which Nikhil progresses is always beyond the claims of Bimala's imagination.

It may be noted that for Gandhi means are everything. He did not believe that there is a serious divide between means and end. In fact realisation of the goal is in exact proportion to that of the means. The end is beyond us but the means are within our domain. Indeed Nikhil, to me, seems to be aware of this means-end ratio. Anti-Machiavellian, he like Gandhi preaches the inseparability of politics and morality. ("Non violence is the law of our species, as violence is the Law of the Brute."[8]) Sandip's Truth stands thoroughly antagonised as Nikhil sanctifies the inviolable bridge between means and the end.

This invariably echoes Aldous Huxley in *Ends and Means*: "'For the means employed inevitably determine the nature of the results achieved; whereas however good the end aimed at may be, its goodness is powerless to counteract the effects of the bad means we use to reach it.'"[9]

At another level, one might say, that a tyrannical glorification of love is to tyrannize a relationship with fear and uneasy agitation. It is a misplaced effort to overreach one's natural self by substituting the false and the infructuous for the true and the substantial. In a way, Nikhil's sternness in objecting to Bimala's argument is a declaration of a freedom from the skewed and warped vision of home and love. Bimala ceases to be an edulcorating mistiness; rather Nikhil begins to see the world with an unclouded clearness. Treading over the vulnerability that ideality in love brews, he unchains himself and discovers a dynamic power that teaches him the 'illimitable energy of freedom.' This is the victory of the *dharma*, the unbending self that never muddles the means-end equation. What can touch the depth and help in the uprush of joy is the harmony between an 'idea' and its balanced realisation; between Bimala as a woman with imperfections and the love that knows to love the imperfections; between the love of a woman as an 'idea' and the love of one's own country as two never conflicting units.

Continuing with the discussion of the means-end relationship, one can notice that Nikhil's Truth has sifted the reason and prudence from the welter of rhetorical nonsense and theoretical exaggeration. Prosperity could be the end but the means to reach it need to be honest industry. Counteracting Sandip's lopsided equation between prosperity and industry, he underlines the pragmatism that leads one to see the dream that industry, not frantic emotion, engenders. He is ready to put money when it is 'industry' that prompts the enterprise; but that one has lighted a fire does not follow that there is food to cook over it. Spending bulk of the money on kindling the fire would not be wise. The wise and the practical mind would think equally, if not more, about the food. The fire, it may be observed, is excitement of the experience, a mere agitation of the mind; to think about the 'food' is wisdom for that would fire up the dream of lighting the fire again. Food is the moral, psychological, social and political force built on reason, sense and with just regard to the reality of the situation; it never allows the value of fire to diminish. The truth of an enterprise and the truth in the value of money come to be realized when the 'fire' is lit to *cook* the 'food' already in place. "Complete renunciation of one's possessions is a thing which very few even among ordinary folk are capable of. All that can legitimately be expected of the wealthy class is that they should hold their riches and talents in trust and use them for the service of the society."[10]

In fact Nikhil's Truth teaches us a voluntary form of socialism that requires self-restraint. He is, to an extent, under the Gandhian principles of charity and generosity whereby keeping the fire and the food of Panchu in sight outweighs the importance to take shares in a cotton mill the revolutionaries wanted to start. In this context the Socratic Chandranathbabu highlights the dignity of human life rejecting *sadavrata.* Human truth is glorified in the doctrine of bread labour. The truth in Nikhil combines the intellectual and the manual labour towards the realization of effective social goals. For him, one can say, *swadeshi* and *sarvodaya* are not mutually contradictory terms. Banishing foreign goods from India, however beneficial they might be, is for Nikhil a little too weak an argument. It is tantamount to a fetish of *swadeshi. Swadeshi* can dawn in the true light when the interests of the millions are taken care of and the implacable interest of the coterie is relegated to the back burner. Here finally, perhaps, the combination of 'fire' and 'food' can be effectively realized. Nikhil's Truth has the moral dilemma that holds the contrary tension between the moral obligations to promote the interest of his fellow countrymen and the service for the best interest of the humanity as a whole. For Nikhil, "Economics that hurts the moral well-being of an individual or nation is immoral and, therefore, sinful."[11] For him, true economics, is never at odds with the highest ethical standard. Industry needs to nourish without impulsiveness and slapdash; money needs to realize its true value with the principle of *sarvodaya* and the spirit of truth.

IV

By imbibing the principles of *sarvodaya*, Nikhil aligns himself with the virtuous and cannot severe his ties from the wicked. He cannot turn Sandip away despite the unacceptability of his principles and philosophy. He believes in the truth of an aspiration for a harmony in man and admits in the same breath the imperfection or disharmony of the world. This need not be interpreted as a compromise. Man, he believes, has to have the heart for possible task without weaving webs of illusions for the attainment of the impossible. Believing in universal humanism, Nikhil can soundly counter Sandip's virulent vehemence to seek the result which belongs to-day.

> "The result I seek," answered Nikhil, "belongs to all time." (162)

This again reminds us of Tagore's essay on Gandhi.

> Politicians plume themselves on being practical and do not hesitate to ally themselves with the forces of evil, if they think that evil will accomplish their end. But tactics of this kind will not pass the audit of the Dispenser of our fortunes; so while we may admire their cleverness, we cannot revere them. Our reverence goes out to the Mahatma whose striving has ever been for Truth, who, to the great good fortune of our country at this time of its entry into the New Age, has never, for the sake of immediate results, advised or condoned any departure from the standard of universal morality. (329)

Nikhil's statement—'The strength I believe in is the strength of renouncing'—and the assertion—'The day that we seek the good of the country along the path of righteousness, He who is greater than our country will grant us true fruition'—put his philosophy of action and the faith in the truth of the Harmony in proper light. He uses his conscientiousness to decide his actions. He endorses the principle of participation without suppression; rather an empathetic attitude informs his identification with the processes of the outer world. A study in *voluntas communis* as contrasted with *voluntas propria*, Nikhil's Truth combines contemplation with action that leads to social utility. Tagore is specific on this aspect of social utility.

> We have a greater body which is the social body. Society is an organism, of which we as parts have our individual wishes. We want our own power and licence. We want to pay less and gain more than anybody else. This causes scramblings and fights. But there is that other wish in us which does its work in the depths of the social being. It transcends the limits of the present and the personal. It is on the side of the infinite.[12]

Nikhil is sure-footed about his licence and power for he puts his finger with composure on the inner nerve of our social being without losing the balance between the energy for the finite and the infinite. Buddhaghosha maintains that the person who is strong in energy and faith but weak in concentration and understanding is overcome by distractions, and starts to believe in the 'wrong' objects. Nikhil, under unremitting self-scrutiny, argues without the impository tone against Sandip's game of Truth and Illusion. Passion, for Sandip, is the street lamp which guides us. Any effort to call it untrue is as hopeless as to expect to see better by plucking out our natural eyes. Nikhil accepts the truth of passion but only when the truth of restraint is recognized.

> By pressing what we want to see right into our eyes we only injure them: we do not see. So does the violence of passion, which would leave no space between the mind and its object, defeat its purpose. (72)

Nikhil points out that an intrusion of strength, where strength is out of place, never helps one in his work. This is an implicit pointer to Buddhaghosa's emphasis on balance between energy/faith and concentration/understanding. Lao-tzu maintains that those who have virtue (interpreted here as *dharma*) attend to their obligations and those who have no virtue attend to their claims. Nikhil, as I have shown, adheres to his *dharma* with conviction. His Truth has realized a freedom which is not in the mere sense of independence, it is a harmony of relationship that occurs not out of a mere knowledge or a response to the world in knowing, but through the union of perfect sympathy.

> And yet, where the question is not that of utility but of moral perfection, we hold it important that the individual should be true in his goodness. His outer good work may continue to produce good results, but the inner perfection of his personality has its own immense value, which for him is spiritual freedom and for humanity is an endless asset though we may not know it. For goodness represents the detachment of our spirit from the exclusiveness of our egoism; in goodness we identify ourselves with the universal humanity.[13]

Nikhil, being alien to the laws of an egocentric existence, successfully unites himself with the 'greater current' of humanity. His 'gains' owe it to a well-experimented and disciplined striving for harmony. He realizes his surroundings as his 'larger self' where ambition does not defile it. In the closed world of hard facts, his Truth leads him towards a *mukti* which is a harmony among his disparate selves. So our income must balance the expenditure.

> We must draw in the goods of eternity in order to be able to give out the goods of time. But the goods of eternity cannot be had except by giving up at least a little of our time to silent waiting for them . . . *olium sanctum quaerit caritas veritatis; negotium justum suscipit necessitas caritatis* ('The love of Truth seeks holy leisure; the necessity of love undertakes righteous action.')[14]

Nikhil admits the necessity of 'waiting'—the waiting for the right situation to act and the waiting that is needed for a spiritual emancipation. He stamps his wisdom when he says, "Good fortune comes to our gate and announces itself, only to prove that we have not the power to receive it,—that we have not kept things ready to be able to invite it into our house." (117) In the silent 'waiting,' Nikhil's Truth teaches us the necessity to prepare oneself for the 'worship'—the growing of the power in us to accept His boon. This is a preparation in righteousness, renunciation and tolerance. Sandip fails to prepare himself because he lacks the knowledge of the nature of universal truths and the true self of man. There is a self-alienation in him that alienates him from Truth. Nikhil works under the philosophy of identity and participation. Through the fabric of self-suffering he prepares himself to participate in the service of humanity. His Truth cannot ignore the growth of Bimala under the shade and breeze of his Love (the home) and cannot evade the urge to stand aloof in the highway of the universe to feel 'that he is part of all.' He realises:

> Suffering there must be; but I must save myself, by any means in my power, from one form of self-torture: I must never think that my life loses its value because of any neglect it may suffer. The full value of my life does not all go to buy my narrow domestic world; its great commerce does not stand or fall with some petty success or failure in the battering of my personal joys and sorrows. (78-79)

He is ready to suffer all, knowing all, with eyes open. He advocates the way of renunciation *in* action, karma yoga, rather than renunciation of action. His morality is at dissonance with the morality of utilitarianism. He cannot gain his success at the cost of the soul for soul is greater than success. Nikhil believes that the soul knows itself in the infinite and transcends its success. He asseverates: "Where our country makes itself the final object, it gains success at the cost of the soul. Where it recognises the Greatest as greater than all, there it may miss success, but gains its soul." (101) This reminds us of what Tagore said in *The Modern Review*:

> The wakeful ageless God of India calls to-day on our soul—the soul that is measureless, the soul that is undefeated, the soul that is destined to immortality, and yet the soul which lies to-day in the dust, humbled by external authority, in the fetters of blind observances. With blow upon blow, pang upon pang, does he call upon it. *atmanam viddhi*, know thyself. (Sept. 1917, p. 339)

Indeed through his insistence to save the soul, Nikhil tries to subordinate the 'brute' nature to the truth of Man and the life current of universal humanity. Man, to Nikhil, is neither mere physiology, nor biology, nor even sociology. "For God's sake don't forget that Man is infinitely more than the natural science of himself. . . . You want to find the truth of man from your science teachers, and not from your own inner being." (73) This again echoes Tagore in 'Man's Nature.'

> Our physical life realizes its growing meaning through a widening freedom in its relationship with the physical world, and this gives it a greater happiness than the mere pleasure of satisfied needs. We become aware of a profound meaning of our own self at the consciousness of some ideal of perfection, some truth beautiful or majestic which gives us an inner sense of completeness, a heightened sense of our own reality. This strengthens man's faith, effective even if indefinite—his faith in an objective ideal of perfection comprehending the human world. His vision of it has been beautiful or distorted, luminous or obscure, according to the stages of development that his consciousness has attained. But whatever may be the name and nature of his religious creed, man's ideal of human perfection has been based upon a bond of unity running through individuals culminating in a supreme Being who represents the eternal in human personality.[15]

In this, Nikhil's Truth realizes the true meaning of existence and civilisation, not by cleverness and possession but by the power of his dharma that unites with an inherent rhythm that transmutes facts to truth without forgetting the eternal Presence that gives an innate sense of completion. The sense of a 'deeper being' opens his mind to the greater unity of the world and the eternal reality of Man. He could create his own 'music' that outgrows the mere superfluity of possessions and progresses towards a Harmony that has no room for unruly passions. He comprehends the misery of being bound up with things lesser than him. Tagore writes: "It is only when a man truly realizes what his possessions are that he has no illusions about them; then he knows his soul is far above these things and he becomes free from their bondage."[16]

Nikhil realizes his possessions and achieves a harmony that teaches him to differentiate between the complete man and the merely useful man; it infuses a rhythm that is built on assimilation and restraint. He has a sense of life, a sense of inner life, the gift to be natural with nature and human with human society, leading him to the 'further world of freedom.'

V

In contradistinction to Sandip, who has submitted himself to obsessive unreason, Nikhil reposes his faith in the Eternal Law.

> When in that midnight, standing under the silent stars, I looked upon that figure, my mind was struck with awe, and I said to myself: "Who am I to judge her? O life, O death, O God, of the infinite existence, I bow my head in silence to the mystery which is in you." (226)

It is the world's great order existing with a happy zeal and unique limpidness. It is what provides the 'peace' and accords value to the 'tears.' Tagore has marked a vital system of cadence, a reticent grace of self-control when exuberance is not a malady of exaggeration, but a blessing. The system (I interpret it as harmony) supplies the modulations of life and unreason readily ceases.

> in the infinity of human spirit,
> and in that dim-lighted dawn
> she speechlessly gazes through the break in the mist
> at the vision of Life and of Love
> rising from the tumult of profound pain and joy.[17]

In Nikhil's submission to the Powers rings the cry: "More strictly, then, the inward judge obey!"[18] His truth approximates the Emersonian truth in the sense that when all things work exactly in accordance with their quantity and quality, it is man with his pretensions, wishes and attempts things beyond his force. This is also a submission to an order of Freedom that allows life to live amidst Justice. One's life is not solely one's own. The Harmony injects an urgency to express some great idea in the process of giving shape to one's life on the lines suggested by the Creator. The 'shaping up' should be with the help of the 'surroundings.' In understanding the religion of man, Nikhil disclaims any form of tyranny both within and without. He understands the futility of trying to mould his relation with Bimala in a hard, clearcut, perfect form. He needs to free her to win her. Creation has its freedom and tampering with it meets with a bitter backlash. In his self-creation and self-experimentation, Nikhil does not ignore the freedom of the individual self and the flexibility of the greater self, which includes the 'environment' and the 'universe.' As a man of liberated spirit, his *is* is under scrutiny as he strives towards his *to be.* He receives the vital spark and can shake off the stigma of not being able to impart only at the end when he gallops away without a weapon. In fact the 'vitality' in him rises out of the stupor of moral dilemmas to gallop into the open.

> To-day, all the ramparts of the dark night
> are crushed under the dust.
> To the call of the new life

come reassuring echoes
from the peaks of the sunrise
'Fear not, fear not!
Victory, victory, victory, to resurrected man,'
echoes the cry across the mighty heavens.[19]

Having acquired his inner freedom and harmony, he proceeds to pacify the ignorant army clashing by night. He has his principle of *ahimsa* (symbolized by his disregard for weapon) and sacrifice that keeps the spark alive inside him. He understands that

. . . those who clung to their homes
are doomed to lie perpetually encased in
the shell of a rigid life
in a soulless world. "Along Time's Chariot-Path"

Here Bimala is a bundle of contradictions and distractions which is aptly symbolized by her inability to leave the window and act. The acuity of Nikhil's remark—'What I want is, that I should have you fully in the outside world. That is where we are still in debt to each other'—is more stabbing here than anywhere else. The window stands to relate her ineffectively with the home and the world and her inaction is the acknowledgement of the hiatus between the two poles. Nikhil's fatal injury is no destruction but a Hope for reconstruction on an 'idea' grounded in freedom of the home and the world. His injury is a pause for men to self introspect and separate the 'vital' from the vicious in life. His injury is meaningful as he 'dies into the fulness'[20] and Amulya's death is a glaring pointer to the failure of Sandip's passionate music. His Truth has come to distinguish what is in him from what he foolishly imagined to be his possessions. It is a discovery of the harmonious self that is not crippled or sick to be nursed on the invalid diet of unruly passion and illusions; it is a spirit which has the 'substance' to go through the rigours of trials and come out victorious. The harmony of the spirit renders the 'home' into a world and the 'world' redefines its entity as the encompassing home. The quest can finally be considered to have reached its consummation.

NOTES

1. Rabindranath Tagore, *The Home and the World* (Macmillan, 1992), pp. 44-45.
2. Ralph Waldo Emerson, "Self-Reliance," *Selected Essays*, ed. Larzer Ziff (Penguin Classics, 1985), p. 177.
3. Qtd. in Herman Frankel, *Early Greek Poetry and Philosophy*, trans. Moses Hadas & James Willis (Basil Blackwell), 1975.
4. *The Way of Life* (According to Laotzu), trans. Witter Bynner (Poetry London, 1946), p. 60.
5. *The Selected Works of Mahatma Gandhi* (Ahmedabad, 1968), vol. VI, p. 436.
6. *Ibid.*, Volume Vl, p. 156
7. "Mahatma Gandhi," *Boundless Sky*, Rabindranath Tagore (Calcutta: Visva Bharati, 1964), p. 331.
8. *The Selected Works of Mahatma Gandhi*, Volume Vl, p. 156.
9. Aldous Huxley, *Ends and Means* (London: Chatto & Windus, 1941), p. 52.
10. M.K.Gandhi, *All Men Are Brothers*, p. 137.
11. *The Selected Works of Mahatma Gandhi*, Volume Vl, p. 321.
12. Rabindranath Tagore, *Sadana* (Macmillan, 1979), p. 68.
13. Rabindranath Tagore, *The Religion of Man* (London: Unwin Books, 1970), p. 121.
14. Aldous Huxley, *The Perennial Philosophy* (Flamingo, 1994), p. 362.
15. Rabindranath Tagore, *The Religion of Man* p. 91.
16. Rabindranath Tagore, *Sadana*, pp. 130-31.
17. Tagore, "Ageless Light."
18. Matthew Arnold, "The Better Part."
19. Quoted from Sarvepalli Radhakrishnan's essay 'Most Dear To All The Muses,' in Rabindranath Tagore 1861-1961 (New Delhi: Sahitya Akademi, centenary volume, 1961), p. xxiv.
20. Rabindranath Tagore, "Fruit Gathering LIV" (Macmillan).

Bimala: A Consistent and Developed Point of View on Feminism

KEYA MAJUMDAR

Florescent in the light of her intellectual self-appraisal, razor-sharp to the point of hurtingly honest self-examination, grounded in the threshold of the home yet flying high in the open horizon of the outer world: Bimala's character is the centrepoint in Tagore's novel, *Ghare Baire* (1916). Comprising three characters only, the docile-turned-smart Bimala; her husband Nikhilesh: the quiet, generous but cold intellectual; her husband's friend, Sandeep: the fire brand sophist, the story moves through autobiographical self-searching of all the three characters in the context of the Swadeshi Movement. In fact, Swadeshi is the backdrop against which the three characters play and interplay with or against each other with conflicting emotions, illusions and disillusionment.

During the first decade of the twentieth century, women liberation was becoming more and more the focal point of the Bengali society. In fact, Vidyasagar, Rammohan Roy and Viveka-nanda had already started to think and act constructively about this issue right from the nineteenth century. In literature also, Bankimchandra, Saratchandra and Tagore took up the cudgels against all the rotten and biased views of the patriarchal society. While Bankim idealized the issue, Saratchandra's utmost concern for the ever-deprived womenfolk inclined to be rather subjective and emotional. Tagore, however, looked at the issue with objective curiosity and psychological probity. Tagore's fine artistic sense and intellectual analysis of the "felt" anguish of the character prevents the character from wallowing in solipsistic self-pity. He has given Bimala all the space she needed, more space indeed than that of the other two male characters. Like her husband and her lover, she too has a point of view which is deeply rooted in her own realization of what is right and what is wrong. And if she vacillates between the two, she never leans against any protective idealism, or, escapes into the romantic shadows of any colourful configuration. She faces the situation unfazed. Nor does she ever show any tendency to take refuge in cowardly self-justification. No Prufrockian diffidence on her part to sing the love song. She takes the plunge in engaging herself in an affair outside marriage, with full knowledge of the loving and generous husband. Her point is not to deviate from the designated path of the wifehood just for liberation's sake. She was living a fairly content life hitherto, quite pleased with herself. When the revelation bursts upon herself about a vital emptiness in her own being, she acknowledges and recognizes this other, very important, hidden self of the Womanhood. This new-found identity of her would not now remain suppressed by her duty-bound, wifely, devotional role-acting. Sandeep sweeps her off her feet literally from her false pretences, and kindles into her the flame of free thinking. Gradually taking shape along the course of the novel, her character develops, with her courage and her reasoning capability acting as corner-stones on which her strong point-of-view gets based. She analyses herself correctly thus, when she says, "Whatever I did or thought [regarding Sandeep] was almost unconsciously done or thought by me as if the whole of my nature was working within me on its own accord." (My translation) The tone is not rebellious, but, reflective. Knowing the nature of her inner being, accepting it and its outcome with the same objective detachment is where the strength of the character lies.

The first stirring of unrest in her apparently placid, homely life of a wealthy, respectable landowner's wife was visible with countrywide awareness about Swadeshi Movement, and Sandeep's fiery speeches about patriotism. As she says, "I became restive as I could hear distinctly the clarion-call from the far horizon standing on the fence of my household, the fence that I had erected up so lovingly along my home with so much effort and desire."

Right from this moment, the dramatic conflict starts in her character, and, as she finds herself getting more and more embroiled in her personal relationship with Sandeep, her inner turmoil also increases by degrees. She can, however, easily ignore her sister-in-law's pointed comments, as she has known all these years, the vacuous, envious and supremely narrow attitude of the uneducated womenfolk, whose interest of life circles round the household chores and tongue-slashing.

Juxtaposing the educated, perceptive and self-questioning character of Bimala, against the stupidly self-complacent idler sister-in-law, Tagore has brought in focus the real place of the enlightened woman in the household as well as in the society. But the point which is more important to note, is, the dramatic juxtapositioning of Bimala's devoted-to-duty outlook (for the husband) against the dedicated-to-passion urge. Here is the totally changed perspective of Bimala, from which her strong point-of-view emerges. And again there is the juxtaposition of Bimala's passion for the liberation of the country from the oppressive British rule, and very personal passion for the charismatic image of macho male, Sandeep, who brazenly declares,

> I must have the one whom I desire. Subtlety be hanged. I must get hold of her with my two strong hands. Whatever comes between will be broken to pieces, will be crushed to dust, will be flown over to winds,—this is the ecstasy I'm looking for; this is the Tandava of Reality, after which life and death, good or evil, weal or woe are of no value, no value at all.

Her passion runs towards this aggressive spirit, whereas the pure gentlemen, intellectual husband gets his quota of duty and compassion only. And chasing this closely follows her self-flagellation also. Thus giving required space for development for each aspect of her character, and allowing her to find her way out of the jumbo jumble that she has created for herself, Tagore has very patronisingly and subtly given voice to the needs and cries of feminism in the perspective of his time and place. The adulterous strain of the story has been soft-pedalled keeping in view the castigating finger of the prevalent societal mores maybe, but Tagore, it seems, was more concerned to let the character of Bimala gain its full dimension as a free woman in every sense.

True feministic spirit lies not in bland and blank revolution, or, in negating the existing norms, but in the urge to express itself with total freedom. Revolution lies not in fighting the society for fighting's sake, but to find outlet for every suppressed urge and inspiration. And the courageous spirit of feminism lies in the boldness to accept the consequences after analysing every disturbing nuance, every puzzling instinct of one's own self. Like mysteries of life, Bimala's story also does not have a prim and proper conclusion as such. As the novel ends, we find her at the threshold of her home vis-a-vis another conflict. She is not sure whether she gets the husband back, who had set her free; or would she ever get Sandeep back, whom she had set free. With this dangling question Tagore has let Bimala to fight her way out.

It had not been easy for her. From a nonchalantly devoted wife, to obsessedly infatuated love-sick woman, to the conflict-torn, disillusioned, sadder but wiser human being—her journey from her home to the world outside, from Nikhilesh to Sandeep specifically, is the bumpy mental journey through thorny thoroughfare of doubts, raptures and regrets. Ostensibly, her journey outward her home is to work for freedom movement with Sandeep, as cunningly Sandeep the opportunist, takes this as a pretence to take her along the way of his own romantic overtures and carnal desires. And, all the time he makes it a point to eulogize her inner beauty. Bimala was very conscious of the fact that she was not beautiful by common standard. But Sandeep calls her "Queen Bee," as she is the centre of all their patriotic activities. And Bimala readily starts to believe in this panegyric, because her freedom loving soul was hungry for its recognition for its own sake—not just as an appendage to the very respectable, very generous, very wealthy

Nikhilesh. Sandeep manipulates his erotic advance with shameless flattery, and as her dormant passion runs over to the point of distraction she is drawn blindly to the tantalizing temptation of carnal desire. But at that very moment she explores herself and saves herself with an instinct.

This is her mother's instinct, the third dimension of her character. For Amulya, the teenage boy, who works for Sandeep with dreams in his eyes, her motherly affection overflows. She is saved from the impending doom as she defies Sandeep to lead Amulya to the right path. Here is another shade of her feministic spirit that is fed by extra courage and determination from her calm and placid mother-instinct as the turbulent lover's instinct gets easily overpowered.

The seed of her disillusionment with Sandeep's romantic image starts germinating now. Even so, she cannot yank herself free altogether and totally from the evil influence of Sandeep. Hence comes her helpless confession, "Even so, this lute of mine made with flesh and blood, emotion and feeling, started ringing by the stroke of his hand. I detest that hand. I despair this lute, But how can I ever deny the fact, that this lute of mine is attuned to him only."

As Sandeep's magnetic charm forces her to pilfer money from her husband's coffer, she hates Sandeep more for it. But she has the guts to make this plain confession that Sandeep can and has awakened her dormant passion the way her husband had never done. Both the men love Bimala and Bimala too loves both of them in her own special way, and what makes her viewpoint feministic, is that it was upto her to decide her own course of emotion and action. Plumbing deep down into the wreckage, as well as puzzlingly beautiful mysteries of the sub-conscious, and giving both of them equal importance before judging them on her scale of objective reasoning, she takes her decision. This indiscriminate clarity of purpose sans self-pity is the strong base of feminism in any given time and space. Following the concept of "Know Thyself" Bimala dares to "know" herself leaving no stone unturned in that mysterious cave of existence. Also, by this process of examining, interrogating and studying the impregnable mysteries of her restless mind and heart she wants to transgress and transcend all her torturous experiences.

She is struck by her realization of Sandeep's reciprocation. As she says she cannot help loving him so it seems the case with Sandeep too. After all the false pretences, loud-mouthed proclamations, et al, he too seems to have the thorn of love embedded deep in his heart—inextricably. He almost talks to himself addressing his Queen Bee though, "Queenie, for the first time in my whole tempestuous life I am haunted with a persistent 'But.' I have spent sleepless nights to struggle with it but it has come out victorious all the time demanding its share. Even a rogue like me cannot avoid this pull of demand."

Will her split personality clearly divided between the husband, whom she 'worships' and Sandeep, to whom she is attracted inexorably, be ever unified into one? Can her 'heart' be wiped clean like a tabula rasa—by coming back to square one? We are sharply reminded of another strong-willed feministic character of Shaw, Candida, who after similar conflicting situation decides to come back to her 'weak' husband, and the jilted poet's mystery remains the unsolved mystery as he melts out in the enveloping darkness. Tagore clearly is not interested in proclaiming any final solution to Bimala's problem simply because there cannot be any panacea solution to such problem. The moot point is, how strong the values of the person are to combat unendingly with such conflicting issues, and how the person faces the war within oneself. In this context, Bimala's strong character comes out winner, and here is the triumph of her sensible, mature womanhood. In her self-appraisal as stream of consciousness, divided in seven parts as Bimala's autobiography, Tagore has shown her consciously breaking down the barriers and the stereotypes enforcing a new perspective.

In view of the common theme of the struggle of passionate love for forbidden against the docile love of monotonous domesticity, the struggle of individual aspiration against the common norms of society—Tagore's Bimala stands apart from Anna Karenina or Catherine Earnshaw or Jane Eyre, for that matter. She neither kills herself like Anna did, nor deludes herself like Catherine did, nor tries to strike a compromising balance as Jane Eyre did. She just faces it all—all the gore and glory. This feministic courage of Bimala reminds one of Lavanya, another strong willed, solidly realistic, powerful female character of *Shesher Kabita* of Tagore. But Lavanya's feet are solidly grounded on day-to-day practical reality, and the conflict of the warring selves is more acute in Bimala undoubtedly, because of her yearning for the unattainable.

Tagore never did assume the role of social reformer, pronouncing expiation or providing extenuation for the so-called sin of his heroines, i.e., Damini, Binodini, Charulata. All of them preferred to love the person outside matrimonial convention. While hinting at the impregnable mystery of love, he did imagine correctly the terrible conflict that these women had to undergo, protecting their social status and protecting their 'love' all at once. With the humanistic outlook and intensity of Tolstoy and Dostoevsky, Tagore has never failed to give the accurate picture of the world and power of mind and need over social customs and norms, taking the reader through chiaroscuro of the feminine heart with utmost ease and elan. He empathizes perfectly with all these women's states of mind as his sharp perception would try to find out the psychological pressure unique to each character under the influence of which they behaved the way they did. And, then, his artistic self would place them in context, consciously trying to give a form and utterance to the long neglected sentiments, emotions and helpless situations of these stereotyped women. He dares to take a sharp turn in portrayal of these women characters, especially Bimala, as no one equals her elastic self-judgement and piercing self-analysis.

From the scores of shoddy, dependent, self-effacing, foolishly-sacrificing women, he had etched out Damini, Kumu, Lavanya, Charu or Bimala with fixed identities of their own which they fight for. In this long journey from self-suppression to self-accentuation Bimala is undoubtedly the pioneer. Her husband's care and concern and utmost devotion for her could not fulfil the vacuous emptiness within her, that Sandeep's passionate eulogies had created. So desperately she clings to Sandeep, not for the romantic illusion of love only, but more importantly for the solid base of her identity, as she clearly points out, "I need Sandeep in my world to know and feel the value of my identity."

Another attribute of feminism that we find in Bimala, is the ideal welding of typical Indian values with Western open-mindedness. To have the complete freedom of mind and intellect from age-old taboos and rotten tradition Bimala had to walk through fire. Her European education from Ms. Gilby inspired her to be open-minded, progressive and courageous. On the other hand her mother was her loving role-model whose typical Indian values she had tried to imitate in her married life. Striking a balance between the two to forge out a definite and viable womanhood, seems to be the motto of the novelist for Bimala.

Nikhilesh committed the mistake of disregarding the demands of this persistent womanhood of Bimala. He just took her for granted, and, did not care much for Bimala the Individual. He was so engrossed in his own ideal of loving the romantic idea of love. Bimala was supposed to be a mute recipient of all the favours and the effusive paraphernalia of romanticism. He missed all the signs of eager, personalized offerings of Bimala's heart, that wanted to give back her share fully complementing what she received. Hers was not a meek and content personality that would remain pleased with her quota of rationed attention. The strong feministic undercurrent of her character wanted her womanhood to be established with all its glory, and her recognition as Bimala the woman only. Sandeep touched her with livewire at this vulnerable point. Her passion for Sandeep, her respect for her husband, her contempt for the mean and meek woman-gossip, her motherly concern for Amulya, her real urge to work for Swadeshi,—all these colours of her character are beautifully mingled to reflect and refract through the prism of her ever-mystic womanhood: strong as well as subtle, Bimala's step into the outside world from the confines of home symbolizes a very decisive step of the early twentieth century enlightened woman, to shape her destiny with her own hands.

The Polarized World of *The Home and the World*

NANDITA SINHA

The Swadeshi movement sweeping Bengal in the years between 1905 and 1911 forms the background of Tagore's novel, *Ghare Baire* (*The Home and the World*).[1] The novel also probes into the individual sensibilities and personal conflicts of the three main characters, the enlightened and sensitive zamindar, Nikhilesh, his wife, Bimala, whose foray into the world outside the cloistered shelter of the Zenana brings about catastrophic consequences, and the flamboyant and unscrupulous pseudo-nationalist and revolutionary, Sandip. The novel presents the complexities of a particular political period—its grandeur and its pettiness, its triumphs, problems and tragedies, all seen in relation to the lives of particular individuals.

Rabindranath had actively participated in the campaign against Lord Curzon's proclamation of the partition of Bengal in 1905 and written patriotic songs. He had joined the movement with zealous hopes, but within a few months he turned away disillusioned. He found the revolutionary gospel to be geared towards destruction, while his own instinct was for reconstruction. His ideal was harmony, not division. "Boycott," the key concept of the revolutionary doctrine meant rejection of Western goods, yet there was no corresponding impulse towards the viable manufacture of indigenous goods nor was there an effort to form an educational system that would substitute for the foreign one. Rabindranath deplored the mindless violence and hysteria that very soon became adjuncts of a movement that had originally been meant for political protest as a means of gaining freedom and nationhood. The young terrorists who threw bombs with shouts of Bande Mataram were deluded into believing that this was the way to end foreign domination, but without a programme of national upliftment, their enthusiasm became misdirected sloganeering and aggressiveness. As Bimala puts it in the novel: "We had no distinct vision . . . the new epoch came in like a flood, breaking down the dykes and sweeping all our prudence and fear before it." (22) Rabindranath sensed the dangers of uncontrolled enthusiasm. He saw responsibility veer away towards unprincipled attainment of selfish ends, the balance lost between nationalism and communalism. In the novel, he shows Nikhilesh horrified as he sees the political conflict turn into racist violence, embodied in the attack on the defenceless Englishwoman, Miss Gilby. He gently reminds Bimala that her sudden feelings of hostility towards a woman who loved her, merely because she was English, was unfair. Chandranath Babu, the wise old teacher, sums it up succinctly: "I see no good in this," said he, "this setting aside of conscience and putting the country in its place." (224)

In *Ghare Baire*, Tagore makes a sharp distinction between rival impulses: in Nikhilesh, he creates the champion of truth, who refuses to pass off "injustice as a duty and unrighteousness as a moral ideal." (38) He thinks of the country in terms of the poor and the downtrodden, whom he wants to raise to a better life. Freedom, for him, is linked with idealism. His inherent integrity expresses itself in his refusal to tyrannize his tenants into abjuring foreign-made articles. He himself adopts the swadeshi creed in a practical manner in his day-to-day life, sharpening his Indian-made pencils with his Indian-made knife, writing with reed pens, drinking water out of bell-metal vessels, working at night in the light of an old-fashioned castor-oil lamp and using an ordinary brass pot as a flower vase instead of imported crystal. But nobody, except the Bara Rani, either understands or sympathizes with him, and even Bimala dismisses "this dull, milk-and-water Swadeshi" as unappealing.

On the other hand is Sandip, whose dominant trait is greed in the guise of nationalist fervour, who cloaks his ulteri-

or motives and shallow self under the garb of patriotic jingoism. He represents Illusion as opposed to Truth. For him, moral ideals are illusions, to be discarded as soon as they cease to serve his ends. Sandip's philosophy shamelessly advocates hate and injustice as incendiary agents to all great action. Pity he equates with cowardice and greatness with lies and treachery. He says, "We must be unswervingly unreasoningly brutal. We must sin." (40) He asserts the power of naked will, of force and greed as the realities of life. He describes himself as belonging to "the flesh-eaters of the world, we have teeth and nails; we pursue and grab and tear." (52) The terms he uses are of plundering, plucking, killing, grabbing. Sandip's inclination for the violent, the brutal and the passionate, extends to his conception of woman. He feels it is man's mission to be "aggressive, to stir up the latent disquiet in her personality." (153)

Bimala becomes the battleground for the clash between these opposing attitudes. The Swadeshi agitation provides the catalyst which propels the sheltered wife from the seclusion and stability of the home to the outer world that is already seething in a political turmoil. Nikhilesh, the liberal, loving husband, wants Bimala to know and experience the freedom of the larger world, to allow her personality to flower and thus to enrich and deepen their love and understanding of each other. But he has not reckoned with the force that Tagore elsewhere calls "the passion which knows neither pity nor trust nor modesty nor shame."[2] As we see her being swept off her feet under the hypnotic spell of Sandip's rhetoric, as her fascination overpowers her genuine devotion for her husband, as we see her undergo stages of exaltation, distress, revulsion and remorse, the nature of the conflict is clearly shaped by the psychological undercurrents that surface. Though she tries to rationalize her agitated feelings as merely a variation of the stormy passion outside which swept the country, she is possessed by a vague, unfathomable yearning which she cannot quite analyse, but which hints at some sexual dissatisfaction. Bimala takes pride in her husband's virtuous behaviour, but somehow cannot get over the feeling that rectitude and manliness do not go together. Her desire is not so much for goodness as for virility, full-blooded passion. And it is this that Sandip has in full measure, along with an astute awareness of the truth of the relationship of the couple. He realizes her satiation with the monotony of placid happiness, that she is "burning in every vein with life-fire" which cannot be kept cool for long "with the wet towel of moral precepts." (67) But he also knows that for women like Bimala, illusions are important and that a convenient avenue for refuge and self-deception must be provided. For this, he takes recourse to what Nikhilesh calls "the hypnotic texts of patriotism." (37) With insidious shrewdness, he directs Bimala to a conception of herself as a divine goddess as Shakti, as an embodiment of Universal Joy. (126) In a moment of clarity, she sees this delusion for what it is. "When, in Sandip's appeals, his worship of the country gets to be subtly interwoven with his worship of me, then does my blood dance indeed and the barriers of my hesitation totter. . . . I feel that my resplendent womanhood made me indeed a goddess." Despite this, her words take on associations of divinity: "Sandip's hungry eyes burnt like the lamps of worship before my shrine," (56) "Divine strength had come to me." (57) She is aware that she is being deluded, but is content to be so. She knows and fears the consequences of this mad infatuation, but is powerless to resist it. All her inhibitions recede before the "cataclysmal desire" (83) and the "mystery of his seething passions, so immense, so tumultuous." (83)

Yet, when realization dawns on her that she has been only used, her shame expresses itself in terms of polarities: "it was the giver of light, of life, of Shakti, of immortality—in that belief, in that joy, I had burst all my bounds and come into the open. . . . Do they want to tell me now that all this was false. The psalm of my praise which was sung so devotedly, did it bring me down from heaven, not to make heaven of earth, but only to level heaven itself with the dust." (196)

To the very end, Bimala remains confused. At one point, she feels free from "the snaky coils" of "his magic spell." (239) She sees Sandip no longer as a king but as a boor. Her relationship with Sandip's innocent, idealistic disciple, Amulya, is instrumental in bringing Bimala to a sense of her role, not as a false concocted image of divinity, but as a real mother and sister. Yet, when Sandip in his final leave-taking, clearly addresses her, not as mother, but as beloved enchantress, she is once again entranced. Now she realizes man's complex nature—that behind Sandip's coarseness, falseness, sensuousness, is something which is beyond understanding—the mysterious forces of creation/destruction, attraction/repulsion.

In the last chapters of the novel, the two main characters reach a stage of introspection and isolation, very near despair. Bimala doubts whether she can ever return to the fullness of her earlier life; whether even God, who can create new things, can create afresh that which has been destroyed. (225) Nikhilesh expresses the truth of his situation in terms of opposites: "To try to keep Bimala as a garland would have meant a weight hanging over my heart." (178) He realizes the "unconscious tyranny" and "despotism" in his desire to mould his relations with Bimala into "hard, clear-cut, perfect form" (272) so that "Bimala's life, not finding its true level by reason of my pressure from above, has had to find an outlet by undermining its banks at the bottom." (272)

The sharp lines of the dichotomy blur a little towards the end, as each character realizes the difficulty of categorization, since all are only wayfarers on the path of life, that beyond the home and the world is the endless current of universal life. (256) But the climax of the story clinches the polarization of attitudes that forms the core of the novel. Sandip, for all his rhetoric, escapes from the holocaust he himself has fomented, while Nikhilesh, translating his idealism into action, rushes unarmed to protect his tenants and their womenfolk in his personal battle against intolerance and oppression.

NOTES

1. R.N. Tagore, *The Home and the World*, Eng. trans. of *Ghare Baire* (Macmillan: India Paperbacks, 1992).
2. S.C. Sengupta, *The Great Sentinel: A Study of Rabindranath Tagore* (Calcutta: A. Mukherjee & Co., 1948), p. 215.
3. See also, Bhabatosh Chatterjee, *Rabindranath Tagore and Modern Sensibility* (O.U.P, 1996).

From Illusion to Self-Awareness: A Study of *The Home and the World*

INDIRA BHATT

Tagore, the Nobel prize awardee for *Gitanjali*, has always eclipsed Tagore the novelist and dramatist. That his novels, short stories and drama have a poetic, lyrical touch is vastly evident. But the dramatic situations a human being faces in life are lost sight of and only his poetry is appreciated and admired. Following Bankimchandra and Saratchandra, Tagore too attempted the novel form but he differed from them in the sense that his novels present reformist tendency through the Rebel in Man against the political and economic situations in India of the time. He blends together the social, political and personal aspects in his characters. He has the wider social and political perspective with a prophetic vision of life that rises above the ordinary.

His characters in *The Home and the World* make their final choices after journeying through illusions and experiences. It is a story of love torn between societal norms and personal cravings, between idealism and realities, between temptations and truth. The three major characters in the novel—Bimala, Sandip and Nikhil—all have their beliefs conditioned by their upbringing, social circumstances and education. Conditioned as they are by their societal norms and traditions they live a life trapped by self-created illusions. This paper attempts to examine how these characters step out of the trappings of illusion through their experiences of realities of life and attain self-awareness.

The Home and the World is a simple story narrated

through the three characters in their own words. The novel thus has a multiple perspective as also a self-confessional autobiographical focus. Tagore has utilized artistically this device to probe the minds of his characters. This device helps the novelist to explore the psyche of the characters, giving them the three dimensional depth. Though they voice to a certain extent the views of the novelist, they are not puppets but flesh and blood creatures. They are the individualistic persona given to choices which they deliberately make.

The novel opens with Bimala's story narrating the events of her marriage to Nikhil with her aspirations to be a model of what a wife should be, as one finds in some epic poems.[1] She is happy to have a fairy-tale prince for a husband in real life, who looks after her with deep love. He arranges for her education, employs a British teacher and introduces her to "the modern age in its own language." Hence he does not expect any devotion or worship from her, on the contrary he bestows upon her his love and devotion: "You showed your love by decorating me, by educating me, by giving me what I asked for, and what I didn't. I have seen what depth of love there was in your eyes when you gazed at me." (20) In her story Bimala confesses that Nikhil's love and lavish devotion made her proud and vain and that she feels she has power over him.

Nikhil wants Bimala to be out of purdah and take interest in the happenings in the outer world. He thinks that the inner world of home does not give any opportunity to his wife to blossom fully, that her full personality would develop if she sees and experiences the world outside: "I would have you come into the heart of the outer world and meet reality. . . . If we meet and recognize each other, in the real world, then only will our love be true." (23) He thinks that "the pressures of society" and household conventions cramp the woman's individuality. Her love for the husband who is the only man she has come across, is incomplete. He is under the illusion that Bimala would continue to love him and in love, trust him fully, even after her exposure in the outer world.

Tagore portrays the life of a woman in purdah in the

Twenties in Bengal upper class society and considers her plight as that of a caged bird. Though he believes in equality of sexes as is seen through Nikhil's eyes, he hesitates little. His portrayal of Bimala is carefully restrained. It appears that he feels time is not yet ripe for the woman to step out and face the real world with all its temptations and cruelties.

It is through Sandip's character that the novelist presents the temptations of life. On the one hand Bimala is given full freedom to mingle with people outside the inner sanctum of home, on the other hand the novelist creates a crafty character like Sandip who lures her by his oratory and tall talks about the work he is doing for the country. She does not understand that "His love for the country is but a different phase of his covetous self-love." (45) He believes that whatever he desires he has a right to acquire and possess. He has a way with women and Bimala believes what he says. She thinks that he is a special person:

> In him was the confluence of millions of minds of the country. When he called me the Queen Bee of the hive, I was acclaimed with a chorus of praise by all our patriot workers. (50)

Sandip makes her feel that she was different. She thinks that "Divine strength had come to me" and that "all the country was in need of me." (50) After this her relations with all the world changes. Once she had thought that Sandip was fleecing her husband. Now she thinks that he is working for a cause and whatever he does, is for this cause of the country. She is also blinded by his praise of her that she has no time to question the right and the wrong of it. She is easily led into deception and considers herself a source of inspiration, as he calls her, "a living flame to guide the patriots in the struggle for freedom." (51)

Living a dream-like existence, considering herself a goddess, her reasoning is clouded with intoxicating admiration that Sandip shows towards her. From the golden letters of wifehood, he leads her into the golden fetters of goddesshood, not realizing that it is deception, illusion that both of them practise. He lures her to believe that she is someone else, a superior being and she does not realize that he is interested in her as a woman and nothing more.

But Nikhil is not deceived. He feels that his love for Bimala would bring her back and she would rise above these temptations of Sandip. He argues that "man is neither mere physiology, nor biology, nor psychology, nor even sociology. . . . Man is infinitely more than the natural science of himself." (61) He debates with himself about his wife, whether she is really his own only because she has married him. What right he has to possess her if she really does not wish to be his? He is the idealist and even if he suffers agony by Bimala's behaviour and Sandip's deceptions, he lets the events take their own course. He does not wish to force Bimala in any way. He observes that "man may be wounded unto death, but he will not die. This is the reason why I am ready to suffer all, knowing all, with eyes open." (61)

Tagore presents in him a tragic trait, and shows how impractical he is in this cruel world of make-believe. He keeps himself aloof and on the fringe of happenings, an observer and yet a sympathizer of Bimala.

But she is not so frank in her dealings with Nikhil. Thinking herself an incarnation of mother-country she though reluctantly gives away the money kept in her treasure box to Sandip and later on her ornaments to Amulya. She dares not ask Nikhil about money, yet she wants to prove to Sandip and to herself that she has power to do what she chooses. It is only when Amulya is caught returning the money that she confesses to have taken it herself. She wants to prove herself independent and courageous. Taking advantage of this, Sandip indirectly compels her to steal from her own treasury in the name of patriotism. Tagore is against the wrong doings, the wrong means for the right cause. He anticipates Gandhiji's philosophy and "warns against the evil means however nobly conceived."[2] Amulya acts as catalyst and Bimala turns back from the path of deception. As K.R.S. Iyenger puts it: "She has to work out her salvation in diligence, through tribulation and experimentation and suffering and disaster, she has verily to go through fire and brimstone before she acquires the discrimination to see the difference between gold and tinsel, between Nikhil who has the innate strength to face a crisis and Sandip who takes to his heels the moment difficulties start." (108)

When Sandip returns her ornaments, the spell of temptation is dispelled and light of realities dawns on her. Tagore portrays Bimala always debating with herself and yet living the world of illusions, of make-believe, of dreams, not knowing the harsh realities of the world outside. Only at the end she wakes up from her dream-like existence and becomes conscious of her wrong doings, her 'sin.' Her experiences of the outer world are not happy. Writing in the Twenties, Tagore thinks that woman could not understand the world of realities which is far more complex and cunning and is not meant for the woman who takes it at its face value. Bimala journeys through the facetious world of Sandip, experiences the deceptions practised by him, and completes a full circle by returning to Nikhil in her repentance. But she is not the same woman who loved him because he was her husband but because he was a man who stood for true love and real freedom. She is free from the tangle of emotional involvement with Sandip and becomes aware of her own true feelings for Nikhil.

Tagore even shows Sandip in a better light at the end of the novel when he boasts of not being repentant. "I am not the man to come back in slobbering repentance to return ill-gotten money," (200) he says. And yet he is a changed man to admit:

> the ghost of compunction has found an entry into my hitherto untroubled conscience. As I have to wrestle with it every night, after my first sleep is over, I cannot call it a phantom of my imagination. (200)

There is no escape for him but to confess his treachery and admit that all his attempts to lure Bimala have failed. Though to Bimala and Nikhil, he reveals himself in true light, Tagore lets him out into the world of freedom struggle implying that in the name of patriotism, many a leader hypnotized the public for their own selfish ends. But Sandip too redeems himself a little bit and realizes that his power over Bimala is illusory and not real.

The Home and the World, set against the backdrop of freedom struggle, Swadeshi movement and the upper class landlords, mirrors the doubts of the intellectuals about the Swadeshi movement, the advantage taken by the feudal lords and the common labour class of society. Against this backdrop the three major characters act out their drama only to prove to themselves their individual realization through their role in this drama of national happenings. Nikhil's quest is for truth, wholesome love, purity and perfection. In this he succeeds but at the cost of his life. Bimala is wavering between the two worlds with one foot outside the threshold of her inner Zanana world. She moves out, only to return to her own known and familiar world. What happens to her after Nikhil's death, one cannot imagine. There is no one left for her to turn to and she must really and truly face the harsh realities of life on her own. One feels that she would not be able to accept 'the caged-bird' status any more. The strength of the novel lies in tracing and depicting the journey of the characters, their conflicts and their arrival at self-awareness. Tagore's novel is more convincing as a psychological study than the novels of Bankim Chandra or Saratchandra.

NOTES

1. Rabindranath Tagore, *The Home and The World* (Penguin Books India, 1999).
2. K.R. Srinivasa Iyenger, *Indian Writing in English* (India: Asia, 1973), p. 107.

The Home and the World: Tagore's Dharma in the Terrain of Desires

VANASHREE TRIPATHY

> Light Oh! Where is the light! Kindle it with the burning fire of desire. It thunders and the wind rushes screaming through the void. The night is black as a black stone. Let not the hours pass by in the dark. Kindle the lamp of love with thy life.[1]

The Home and the World,[2] a deeply autobiographical novel, dramatizes Rabindranath Tagore's participation in the political storm that had gathered over India in the first decade of the century. Tagore's life even while he was in his early youth found itself at the swirling movements of political, social and historical events. In the midst of the intense political awakening for freedom and Swadeshi movement, Tagore opened up some perennial issues of personal as well as public life that even today, at the beginning of the twenty-first sound relevant. As the title suggests, the novel illumines both the 'home' and the 'world' in all their social, psychological, economic, political and metaphysical implications as it portrays the lives of three characters—Bimala, Nikhil and Sandip—in the background of cultural situations of the time and probes into the ephemeral and complex nature of equation between man and woman, the problem of delusion and truth in public and personal lives: the dangerous potentials of the doctrines of Swadeshi, nationalism and patriotism culminating into terrorism.

Tagore strongly criticized the modern world's fascination

with the Western ideology of individualism which, according to him, had grievously harmed human civilization in breeding a narrow concept of nationalism. In *Personality*, he argues: "Men have seen the absurdity of today's civilization, which is based upon nationalism—that is to say, on economics and politics and its consequent militarism. Men have been losing their freedom and their humanity in order to fit themselves into vast mechanical organizations."[3]

The protagonist Nikhil's individualism would like to be in harmony with the common humanity—its fulfilment lies in the egalitarian community of mankind. Nikhil articulates and vindicates Tagore's disillusionment with the Swadeshi cause as he discovers that the movement, which had been conceived to fight the communalist forces set free by the British, had itself become violently communal. His aversion to insane violence and keen interest in the upliftment of the poor masses—in the abject poverty and disarray in the rural areas—is crystallized in the dramatic debates between Nikhil and Sandip. One significant fact that emerges from a close analysis of the debates and the growth of characters and the situations is that the philosophical assumptions and cultural perceptions of life in Tagore may be of the twentieth century, yet the western critical modes of existentialism, modernism and postmodernism may not appropriate them in their deeper connotations and intentions though there may not be any limit to the meaning that the text *The Home and the World* could release in terms of these theories. A powerful alternative to them nonetheless could be found in Indian Dharmic theory that resolves and clearly illuminates most of the relevant issues in the novel which have baffled the western critics.

The core meaning of Dharma is 'that which upholds' or 'that which sustains.' In the belief that Dharma sustains the world, ancient Indians presupposed a natural order inherent in the very structure of life, without which life cannot exist. The *Mahabharata* speaks of ten embodiments of Dharma: *Yasha* or fame, *Satya*, truth, *dama,* self control, *shaucha*, cleanliness, *arjava*, simplicity, *hri*, endurance, *acapalam*, resoluteness of character, *dana*, giving and sharing, *tapas* austerities, and *brahmacharya*, continence. And there are five ways of reaching dharma: *ahimsa*, non-violence, *samata*, attitude of equality, *shantih*, peace or tranquillity, *asteyam*, lack of aggression and cruelty, and *amatsara*, absence of envy.[4] It is important to note that in India's history of social and political ideologies, Dharma has been recontextualized and rehistoricized in Rammohun Roy, Tagore and Gandhi. In *The Home and the World*, Tagore presents his concerns with a vision of India as healthy and vibrant culture and in the characters of discriminating intelligence, acute self consciousness, highly articulate and self aware, one finds a new context, a new revival of Dharma. Anita Desai's comment in the "Introduction" to the novel that "there is nothing static, earth-bound or lifeless about it; it has the complexity and tragic dimensions of Tagore's own time and ours," (8) tells us that in our own time also, the issues taken up in the novel are so closely aligned with the basic and endemic cultural configuration of this country. These issues potently explain themselves in terms of the Dharmic theory of life in relationship with the contemporary world and the novel's protagonist, Nikhil, is one such hero with Tagore's Dharma telling project. In the terrain of desires, Tagore's sacred is posited in the present, not lost in the past that reconnects the contemporary readers with the issues and ideas that always existed, always called for our attention and yet were forgotten. In the twentieth century world, Tagore raises questions and provides possible answers to them in the midst of the Swadeshi movement which sparked off radical imaginings among generations of youth in Bengal and provoked several questions to which the leaders of our country found themselves answerable as history astutely records:

> The weakness of the Swadeshi consisted mostly in its communal implication. There were of course a considerable number of Muslims in the anti-partition [Partition of Bengal 1905] Swadeshi agitation. But the bulk of them was unhappy. There were several conflicts between zamindar officials and Muslim vendors. The poor Muslim peasants could not afford to buy expensive handloom

cloth, the supply of which was in any case limited. Imported cotton textiles were cheaper for them. Subsequent events caused communal riots in East Bengal. Such communal tensions facilitated the birth of the Muslim League in Dacca in October 1906.[5]

Bimala, Nikhil's wife, is torn between the duties owed to husband and the demands made on her by the radical leader of Swadeshi, Sandip. Her first step outside the threshold of the women's chamber, her attempts to resolve the irreconcilable pressures of the home and the world reflect parallel conflict in India combating with the forces of communalism in the home ground while struggling to set itself free from a foreign rule. Its tragic outcome foreshadows the unrest that accompanied partition in 1947.

In Bimala's growing proximity with Sandip and the free floating desire between them, or in Sandip's fatal mixture of truth and falsehood, Tagore does not invest the notion of evil, not in the Christian sense of 'the sovereign evil.' Therefore the conflicting perceptions of Bimala and Nikhil and Sandip and Nikhil do not fall into the category of good or bad. They are rather the mixture of truth and falsehood that pursue all human positions in this universe. Tagore himself was tormented by the paradox that is at the root of creation, a logical contradiction, and in presenting Sandip as one of the three types (*gunas*), the *rajas*, he illuminates the urge of nature, *ucchiṣta*, in him. Sandip's truth in that paradigm is more illusion than truth, for in order to become real, it must be depicted by the infinite that is Nikhil's vision. That infinite lies in penance—in the restraint of *Tapasya*. In his yogi/artist/thinker, Tagore invests the power to seek the truth, but the truth which Nikhil pursues belongs to art and not to science and metaphysics. As a true artist of his Dharma, Tagore transforms himself into multiple questing minds; in all-embracing empathy, he is Nikhil, Sandip and Bimala.

What connects the diverse strands within the vast matrices of the novel and gives it a linear pattern is the growth of the hero Nikhil—his quest and discovery of *Purushartha* in

Dharma, Artha, Kama, Moksha, that also reveal Tagore's notions of internationalism, multipolarties of faith, and respect for the essential freedom of all individuals. In his pursuit of Dharma figure his complex relationship with his wife Bimala and that brings into focus Bimala's volcanic passion for Sandip. In this complicated situation however, Tagore is not trying to find a way between either/or, or the law of the excluded middle or contradiction within human life in terms of either this or that, true or false, reason or faith, man or nature, the individual or society, man as autonomous subject or man as an object. Unlike the history of mentally antagonistic ideologies as in European thought, Tagore is permeated with the awareness of many-sidedness of human life and does not see irreconcilable opposition between aspects of man's individuality and in this mode connects us with both Nikhil, Sandip and Bimala. Corollary to this is Tagore's scepticism of the ascetic abnegation of life. On the issues of moral and spiritual sphere of human existence and the necessity of cultivating our personality in all spheres, he said: "The cultivation of merely the moral side of our nature leads us to the dark regions of narrowness and hardens our heart to the intolerable arrogance of goodness and the cultivation of the merely spiritual side of nature leads us to still darker regions of rivalry in temperance of imagination."[6] The novelist's awareness of this makes the critical task difficult; assigning any one meaning to the pursuit of his characters Nikhil, Sandip and Bimala is problematic.

Nikhil likes to pursue this world as a *Sakshi* (a seer), who would want this world in the process of creating and sustaining individual and social condition when each individual is his or her being, and in relationship with others, is able to explore and test the potential of his or her life. In him, Tagore sees the forger of conscience of his race and from the Dharmic point of view, we find in him the thirteen characteristics of truth, including itself as a predicate, they are equality, self-control, absence of envy, forgiveness, modesty, endurance, not to find faults with others, renunciation, concentration of mind, nobility of conduct, forbearance, and non-violence. Tagore's personal concerns crystallize in the persona of Nikhil. It is a common knowledge that his contempt for selfish and short-sighted nationalism like Nikhil's were grossly misinterpreted in a highly charged political environment of the early twentieth century. Nikhil in *The Home and the World* as a spokesperson of Tagore regards India's problems as social rather than political and attaches more weight to the issues of regenerating India's rural economy, improving her education, reforming her caste-system and improving relation between Hindus and Muslims. It is the Dharma of man: the capacity of man for love, sympathy and creativity that Nikhil truly respected in the world of twentieth century communism and religious fanaticism and the exploitative social hierarchies. Nikhil's re-visioning the true Dharmic objectives of human life and the need for ordering our personal, moral and social relationship in that light is the dharmic mission of *The Home and the World.*

II

The text attains intense dramatic moments in the conflicts of desire that implicate Nikhil with Sandip and Bimala and which have a bearing on their personal and moral convictions. The inner worlds of characters powerfully surface in the point of view of each character and the narrative sensitively registers their relationships to history, culture, politics, and the equations between man and woman. They are the 'reflectors' in the sense Henry James conceived in enunciating his concept of the novels as a "drama of consciousness."[7] In a variation of this mode, "point of view" as a distinct reflection of individual perceptions appears in the diary accounts of Bimala, Nikhil and Sandip. The perspectives of the characters are subtly revealed as Bimala quotes Nikhil on the issues of women's equality and freedom:

> I would have you come to the heart of the outside world and meet reality. Merely going on with your household duties, living all your life in the world of household conventions and the drudgery of household tasks—you were

> not made for that.
>
> If we meet, and recognize each other in the real world, then only will our love be true. (23)

In yet another speech of Nikhil appears the depth and breadth of his character:

> But the man who loves the fish wants to enjoy it in the water; and if that is impossible he waits on the bank; and even if he comes back home without a sight of it he has the consolation of knowing that the fish is all right. Perfect gain is the best of all; but if that is impossible, then the next best gain is perfect losing. (24)

We discern an exposition of Tagore's assumptions about the symbiotic relation into which men and women lost themselves. A few lines from *Gitanjali* express Nikhil's feelings poignantly: "Why did the flower fade?/I clutched it to my heart in excess of feelings and crushed it/Why did the lamps go out?/I shielded it with my clock and it got no air." Nikhil, in defiance of the conventions, would not let Bimala worship him. She quotes him, "Those are cowards who claim absolute devotion from their wives as their right; that is humiliation for both." (13) Bimala's grateful mind recalls the meeting between them, "like the rhyming of a poem; it has to come through the path of metre." (13) Nikhil, studying for M.A., is committed to making Bimala educated and therefore engages Miss Gilby to accomplish this goal. Tagore conveys the view that the repression of women in a society which is authoritarian in its social and sexual codes, which crushes its women beneath the intolerable burden of honour and propriety, breeds repression of other kinds. Nikhil's deep compassion and care for his widowed sister-in-law is also reflective of his comprehensive personality. Bimala had sensed that the senior Rani's claim over her husband was not based merely on our social connection, but went much deeper. (260)

With the arrival of Sandip, and with the palpable growth of intense passion between him and Bimala, Nikhil's idealism has to suffer the anxiety of its contradiction and that pushes him into a situation of dilemma. Nikhil is made to watch in silence suffering Bimala's bashful pride in the magnetic presence of Sandip and the home and the world in this context attain a significant meaning. In setting Bimala free from the confines of home, Nikhil wants to experiment with the validity of his convictions. Even though he may have to face humiliation, he is prepared to come face to face with the truth of human nature that is concealed in the mass of conventions:

> I must not lose faith: I shall wait. The passage from the narrow to the larger world is stormy. When she is familiar with this freedom, then I shall know where my place is. If I discover that I do not fit in with the arrangement of the outer world, then I shall quarrel with my fate, but silently take my leave. . . . Use force? But for what? Can force prevail against Truth? (45)

We get to know that the will to resolve the complication transforms itself into the will to seek liberation from desire with the knowledge that the freedom to which one passes through sorrow is greater than the sorrow itself. Tagore's personal enquiry into the theme of moral imperatives renders itself tellingly in Sandip with equal force. In Sandip's words, Tagore conveys the profound dilemma of his generation's moral position that found itself at the crossroads:

> I was born in India and the poison of its spirituality runs in my blood. However loudly I may proclaim the madness of walking in the path of self abnegation I cannot avoid it altogether. . . . This is exactly how such curious anomalies happen nowadays in our country. We must have our religion and also our nationalism; our *Bhagavadgita* and also our *Bande Mataram*. The result is that both of them suffer. It is like performing with an English military band, side by side with an Indian festive pipe. I must put an end to this hideous confusion. (80-81)

Sandip's role in the novel with reference to the Swadeshi movement as he has aroused the enthusiasm of the masses reveals a kaleidoscope of Machiavellian tactics, Benthamite utilitarianism, Nietzschean and Spencerian individualism. To him personal is also political. He exposes Bimala to a new kind of freedom—the freedom to desire; the right to covet self-fulfilment: "Let her gradually come to the conviction and to acknowledge and respect passion as the supreme reality . . . not to be ashamed of it, not to glorify restraint." (62) His doctrine of the 'survival of the strong man' does not appeal to Nikhil. On this theme Sandip expresses himself:

> Every man has a natural right to possess, and therefore greed is natural. It is in the wisdom of nature that we should be content to be deprived. What my mind covets, my surroundings must supply. This is only true understanding between our inner and outer nature in this world. Let moral ideals remain merely for those poor anaemic creatures of starved desire whose grasp is weak. Those who can desire with all their soul and enjoy with all their heart, it is they who are anointed of Providence, Nature spreads out her riches and loneliest treasures for benefit. They swim across streams, leap over walls, kick open doors, to help themselves to whatever is worth taking. In such a getting one can rejoice; such wresting as this gives value to the thing taken. Nature surrenders herself, but only to the robber. For she delights in this forceful desire, this forceful abduction. And so she does not put the garland of her acceptance around the lean, scraggy neck of the ascetic. (45)

In his eloquent self-congratulatory romantic aggrandizing, Sandip sees himself "as an unexpected bridegroom" in "nature's wedding," (50) and brazenly declares his shamelessness:

> No, I am never ashamed! I ask for whatever I want, and I do not always wait to ask before I take it. Those who are deprived by their own diffidence dignify their priva-

> tion by the name of modesty. The world into which we are born is a world of reality. When a man goes away from the market of real things with empty hands and empty stomach, merely filling his bag with big sounding words, I wonder why he ever came into this hard world at all. (46)

A devotee of desire, he "wants to gorge himself with it to the full." (46)

Sandip received his regular living allowance from Nikhil and as Bimala had become aware even before her encounter with Sandip in Chapter I: "Sandip Babu used to extort money from him on the pretext of Swadeshi work. Whenever he wanted to start a newspaper, or travel about preaching the Cause, or take a change of air by the advice of his doctor, my husband would unquestioningly supply him with the money. This was over and above the regular living allowance." (27) Sandip is not only immoral, but also attractive, virile and charismatic and ironically Bimala now magnetically drawn to him disapproves of Nikhil's moral postures. While enthusiasm for Swadeshi draws Sandip and Bimala together, Nikhil's disappointment with the implications of Swadeshi further estrange Bimala from him. The excited crowds, gloating over bonfires of imported cloth, repulse him; the students who were persuaded and condoled into giving up their schools and colleges to become followers of dubious political leaders make him recognize the waste of their youth and energy. On Swadeshi, he tells Bimala and Sandip, "Why not try to build up something? You should not waste even a tenth part of your energies in the destructive excitement." (27) Bimala, enthused by Swadeshi, resents Nikhil's indifference to this movement and also resents Miss Gilby's presence. She even supports the young boy who insulted Miss Gilby on her way to church. When Nikhil turned the boy out of the house, she could not forgive her husband. Miss Gilby however left the home on her own accord. When Nikhil escorted her to the station, exaggerated accounts of his softness to a white woman give rise to a public scandal which appears in the newspaper,

"Bimala felt that he had been rightly served." (20) These and several other episodes tell us about Nikhil's attitude to the major issues of nationalism and patriotism. His arguments enlarge upon the vacuity of such abstractions. As Bimala reports: "I cannot, my husband said, look upon Miss Gilby through a mist of abstraction, just because she is English. Can't you get over the barrier of her name after such a long acquaintance? Cannot you realize that she loves you?" (28)

While Nikhil resents the jingoism of *Bande Mataram*, works out and plays up the slogan-abstraction of nationalism to the extremes, making Bimala the icon of *Bande Mataram*, the pride of nation. Nikhil treats this euphoria with scorn: "I am willing to serve my country; but my worship I reserve for Right which is far greater than my country. To worship my country as a God is to bring a curse upon it." (29) Tagore's vision of humanity beyond nationalism appears in one of his lectures: "I felt that I had found my religion at last, the religion of Man, in which the finite became defined in humanity and came close to me so as to need my love and cooperation."[8] Nikhil had seen the grim aspect of such short term arousal of patriotic passion and in the subsequent events the narrative shows how the hypnotic power of the wordy slogans and rhetorics enforce a morally wrong idolatry and bigotry on the masses and henceforth ensures an explosive drama of desire and mad passion in personal and public life that explodes in arson, looting and communal riots leading to devastating consequences. Nikhil, Amulya and several other innocent people become the tragic victims of their frenzy.

III

Man and woman, their possibilities and mysteries both intrigued and fascinated Tagore: "Man is as much a mystery to woman as woman is to man. If that was not so, the separation of the sexes would only have been a waste of nature's energy." (145) The concept of female freedom is probed with deeper insight in the complicated theme of triangle in relationship and the impelling nature of desire. In Nikhil, the desire for the visionary quest for truth proceeds from his Dharmic heritage. In Sandip, the desire for power, for female adulation and joy of dark passion burst forth from the volcanic deeps of his nature:

> There is a wrench at my heart, a pang in every nerve. When I have put out the light and am in bed, little touches, little glances, little words flit about and fill the darkness. When I get up in the morning, I thrill with lively anticipations, my blood seems to course through me to the strains of music. (62)

The intricate rhythm of feelings of the characters, Nikhil, Bimala and Sandip, the magnitude of joy, pain, suffering, loss and death retrace the grim and tragic aspects of Rama in the *Ramayana*, Krishna in the *Mahabharata*. In the oldest myth of 'desire' Tagore defines and illumines the ambiguous, tabooed and obscure, and reveals a willingness for an uninhibited absorption of new experiences, new visions and uncanny psychological insight. Commenting on Tagore's aesthetics, Radice remarks: "Tagore is often defined as a man of faith whose art has been dominated by mystical self-realization or spiritual joy; nonetheless his dark tormented paintings have seemed bafflingly at odds with this. But when one studies him deeply one finds that his writings too are full of strangeness."[9] Tagore opens up some radical questions, "can the ritual of marriage bring two people together?" As the truth of *Bhava Srishti* (the creation of feelings) is beyond the social code of marriage, Bimala's attraction for Sandip was a truth that the Hindu society of the early twentieth century found unpalatable. Sandip's growing proximity with Bimala allows the drama of human desires to extend to its extremes and the pulls and pressures of this desire reveal its volcanic forms. Nikhil's desire for intrinsic human values, for the infinite to play its tune within the limits of the finite is sharply contrasted with Sandip's will to power, to steal and to possess a woman's heart and body who is married to his best friend. Every gesture of Sandip evokes the sublime ecstasy in Bimala, the narrative tellingly describes her first confrontation with Sandip when he makes a dramatic entry with his followers:

> Sandip Babu began to speak that afternoon, and the hearts of the crowd swayed and surged; I saw him wonderfully transformed. Especially when his features were suddenly lit up by a shaft of light from the slowly setting sun as it sunk below the roof of the pavilion, he seemed to me to be marked out by the gods as their messenger to mortal men and women.
>
> From beginning to end of his speech, each one of her utterances was a stormy outburst. There was no limit to the confidence of his assurance. I do not know how it happened, but I found I had impatiently pushed away the screen before me and had fixed my gaze upon him. . . . Only once, I noticed his eyes like stars in fateful Orion, flashed full on my face. (31)

And she feels that Sandip must receive the "consecration of a woman's benediction." (31) Meeting his eyes raised tumult of excitement of exaltation in her: "Sandip's hungry eyes burnt like the lamp of worship before my shrine . . . the loudness of his praise, spoken, unspoken, drowned all other voices in my world." (50) Tagore refuses to take a moral posture on this issue, and in Sandip's thoughts appear Tagore's observations of male-female relation. Sandip's proud assumption takes the form of megalomania when he indirectly claims his superiority comparing himself to Nikhil:

> I have found that my way always winds over the heart of women, who are creatures of this world of reality. . . . Women find in my features, my manners, my gait, my speech, a masterful passion—not a passion dried thin with the heat of asceticism, not a passion with face turned back at every step in doubt and debate, but a full blooded passion. It roars and rolls on, like a flood, with the cry: 'I want, I want, I want.' Women feel, in their

> hearts that this indomitable passion in the life is lord of the world, acknowledging no law but itself, and therefore victorious. For this reason they have so often abandoned themselves to be swept away on the flood tide of my passion, seeking naught as to whether it takes them to life or death. This power which wins these women is the power of mighty men, the power which wins the world of reality. (48)
>
> Those who imagine the greater desirability of another world merely shift their desires from the earth to the skies. It remains to be seen how high their gushing fountain will play, and for how long. But this much is certain: women were not created for these pale creatures—these lotus eaters of idealism. (53)

The self tribute of Sandip, the artist of this mundane universe in the phrase 'life blood of the universe' and his reckoning of woman/Bimala as the creative energy invokes the illusion of Shiv-Shakti and also gives the suggestion of a Shavian 'Superman' and woman as the life-force who must find her life mate, and whom the passion of man dried thin with the heat of asceticism or the lotus caters of idealism will not win. (55) The reference is to Nikhil as Sandip conceives him. In his personal life, Tagore always grappled with the personal problems of finding valid answer to the strange affinity between man and woman transcending the barriers of marriage. In Sandip's words are articulated Tagore's personal feelings:

> Affinity! When it suited my need, I have often said that God has created special pairs of men and women, and that the union of such is the only legitimate union, higher than all unions made by law. The reason of it is that though man wants to follow nature, he can find no pleasure in it unless he screams himself with some phrases—and that is why this world is so overflowing with lies. . . . Affinity! Why should there be only one? There may be affinity with thousands. I have discovered means in my own life upto now. . . . She has also dis-

> covered her own affinity to me . . . and then if I do not win, I am a coward. (48)

As argued earlier, Sandip is as much a Tagore as Nikhil is. While most of the time the novelist is compassionate to Nikhil and identifies with him, on quite a few occasions, he distances himself from Nikhil and gives ironic rendering of Nikhil's moral position at stake. Both Nikhil and Sandip share with their writer, a love for the mystic poet Jaideva. Vaishnava love poetry, the amorous lyrics of adoration of divinity, serve as well to express all shades of human passions. In exalting Bimala's aroused passion for himself and his cause, investing her with the symbol of India's freedom, he provides her:

> You're a healthy human being. Your flesh and blood have responded to the call of reality. You are breathing in every vein with life fire—do I not know it? How long should they keep you cool with the wet towel of moral precepts?

The redolent sexual reverberation in the lines indicate an implosive vibration, once adrift is now beyond their control. The force and candour of Sandip's passion—a fact of nature surely disturbed Tagore, a fact that his personal experiences also could not reject. Tagore also relentlessly probes into Nikhil's growing uncertainty and inner darkness as he is made to acknowledge reluctantly: "Her [Bimala's] nature, perhaps can only find a true union with one like Sandip." (65) The subsequent estrangement between Nikhil and Bimala, the loss of love, make Nikhil suffer immensely. Bimala's earlier perception of Sandip in Chapter II, he is "but foppish all over," (30) changes and she finds herself swept off her feet, in her new perception of him as a redeemer of Bengal. In a highly emotive language, the narrative describes Bimala's transformation:

> The storm within me had shifted my whole being from one centre to another. Like the Greek maidens of old, I

> fain would cut off my long resplendent tresses to make a bow-string for my hero. Had my outward ornament been connected with my inner feelings, then my necklet, my armlets, my bracelets would all have burst their bends and flung themselves over that assembly like a shower of meteors. Only some personal sacrifice, I felt, could help me to bear the tumult of my exaltation. (32)

Sandip is a conjurer, an artist of words, to whom Bimala deeply and uninhibitedly responds. She, a connoisseur of his art, undergoes aesthetic experiences generated by *Shringara*, we find in her description of *Chittavaratti, Druti* (melting), *Dipti* (enlightening) and *Vikasa* (expansion)—these three different states are said to result during the course of *rasa* realization. The effect of *Shringara* in the description lies in producing *Druti* (enlightenment) bringing to the fore the inner world of Bimala. Later in Chapter IV, Tagore describes the cataclysmal desire drawing Bimala by day and by night:

> It seemed desperately alluring—this making havoc of myself. What a shame, it seemed, how terrible, and yet how sweet! Then there was my overpowering curiosity to which there seemed no limit. He of whom I knew so little, he never could assuredly be mine, whose youth flared so vigorously in a hundred points of flame—Oh, the mystery of his seething passions, so immense, so tumultuous. (68)

The invitation to Sandip for dinner brings Bimala closer to him. The awareness of Sandip fills her so deeply and consummately that the peeping widow sisters-in-law do not annoy her. It is only the presence of Sandip of which she is conscious. Moreover, Sandip's sharp wit never loses an opportunity to beat Nikhil in arguments. The issue of *Bande Mataram* is one of them:

> So you do not allow that there is room for an appeal to the imagination in patriotic work?

> It has its place, Sandip, I admit, but I do not believe in giving it the whole place. I would know my country in its frank reality, and for this I am both afraid and ashamed to make use of hypnotic texts of patriotism. . . .
>
> But my powers are limited, so my worship of Humanity is continued in the worship of my country.
>
> I have nothing against your worship as such, but how is it you propose to conduct your worship of God by hating other countries in which he is equally manifest? (37)

In Chapter II when Nikhil makes sense of the growing passion between Bimala and Sandip, his desolate lamentation gives us a vague notion of the lack of sexual fervour between Bimala and Nikhil. Could the problems be deeper than Tagore wanted to acknowledge unequivocally! Nikhil asks himself in his loneliness:

> But is strength a mere display of masculinity? Must strength have no scruples in treading the weak underfoot?
>
> But why all these arguments? Worthiness cannot be earned merely by disputing about it. And I am unworthy, unworthy, unworthy. (41)

The novel proceeds from this to the later phase when Nikhil will seek liberation from attachment. In his awakened love for mankind, he recognizes that the true nature of love would be undifferential. He could see through the dangers of "collective egoism" much inferior to the best of which a community is capable. Tagore's belief in "Where the world comes to rest in one nest" in fact was not so much a result of his reading great Western masters but the root of his internationalism or cosmopolitanism were in the eastern tradition. Like his predecessors, Aurobindo and Rammohun Roy in the twentieth century Bengal renaissance, Tagore believed that there must be a realization by the race that only on the free and full life of the individual can its own perfection and permanent happiness be founded. Aurobindo visualized a national culture, a national religion, a national education as useful things—provided they do not interfere with the growth of human solidarity or with individual freedom of thought and conscience; but a state education, a state religion, a state culture are in his views "unnatural violences."

In a range of erudite arguments, both Nikhil and Sandip represent the spirit of the time and in varied versions of truth impel us to identify a difference of convictions which always agitated Tagore's moral sensibility. Responding to this milieu, in his letter to Andrew, he expresses the view that "the idea of non-cooperation is a political asceticism. Our students are bringing their sacrifices to what? Not to a fuller education, but to a non-education. It has at its back a fierce joy of annihilation which in its best form is in asceticism and is worse in that orgy of fightfulness, in which human nature losing faith in the basic reality of normal life finds a disinterested delight in unnecessary devastation, as has been shown in the late war and another occasion which came nearer home to us."[10] Tagore's protest against non-cooperation subjected him to humiliation by the communities of young students and journalists, and reflection of the personal experience unequivocally figures in *The Home and the World* in Nikhil's struggle with the escalating hostility of the educated section of the society. The questions between man and humanity, between the self liberating person and the engrossing collectively are the questions in which human life is poised and these find a Dharmic answer in Nikhil's discussion with his Master, Chandranath Babu, although Sandip has dismissed this reflection as "living in the truth of scriptures" (132):

> One can understand nothing from books. . . . I went on. We read in the scriptures that our desires are bonds, fettering us as well as others. But such words by themselves, are so empty. It is only when we get to the point of letting the bird out of the cage that we can realize how free the bird has set us. Wherever we cage, shackles us with desire whose bonds are stronger than those of iron chains. I tell you Sir, this is just what the world

> has failed to understand. They all seek to reform something outside themselves. But reform is wasted only in one's desires; nowhere else, nowhere else. (134)

Sandip's project of Swadeshi had turned into a self-adulatory self-seeking movement. In the frenzy of collective egoism headed by Sandip, while Muslim vendors find themselves alienated and harassed, poor farmers like Panchu suffer much hardship when looting and arson become a rampant practice of the movement. Sandip's huge demand of Rs. 50,000 further complicates the plot and brings it to the final revelation at a juncture when Bimala's allegiance to the movement intensifies and her hypnotized confidence in her charm and power reaches a climax. She is Durga, the mother goddess. Sandip offers her worship, the revolutionaries bow before her and touch her feet. When Sandip falls at her feet, like "a wave of mighty sea breaking on the shore," she visualizes herself as a goddess of benevolence. In self-aggrandizing moments, she persuades her husband to burn the foreign goods and ironically finds to her shock: "But I could find nothing in him that I could touch. . . . For the first time, a distraught distant look in his eyes—like the desert sky with no merciful moisture of charm, no colour" (137) disturb her.

Nikhil's diary makes us share another direction into which his life was taking him—towards renunciation—the liberation from desire. His moments of despondency and yearning for death, his humiliation, however drive him to deeper introspection, and patient deliberation. The quest for regeneration and salvation makes him assert his true priorities and in the process of rejuvenation, he forgives Bimala and takes care of the matters of his state with courage and singular vision.

The euphoria and frenzy of nationalism grow more clamorous. Amulya's appearance on the scene brings out another facet of Bimala—her motherhood. The discovery of a revolver with him make her sense the sinister intent of the Swadeshi. As a goddess of freedom, she is obliged to help the movement financially. Her devotion to the cause even goads her to steal the money from her husband's treasury; she says: "Sin taints only the weak; I with my *Shakti* am beyond its reach, only a commoner can be a thief" (138); its grim ironic implication however for the first time dawns upon her, and in finding the pistol with Amulya, a young boy, a new change occurs in Bimala for she senses the sinister design behind the movement, and as Tagore describes, the mistress/Preyasi took the place of the mother. In a dramatic epiphany, she could now see Sandip: "and madness naked and rampant danced upon my heart." (141) She realizes the grim potentials of Sandip's part in that desperate orgy in a vision of devastation:

> In this desperate orgy, that gift of five thousand shall be as the foam of wine,—then for the riotous revel! The immovable world shall sway under our feet, fire shall flash from our eyes, a storm shall roar in our ear, what is or is not in front shall become equally dim. And then with tottering footsteps we shall plunge to our death—in a moment all fire will be extinguished, the ashes will be scattered, and nothing will remain behind. (142)

Sandip's insolent demand for money forces Bimala to steal money from the treasure and makes her feel ashamed. When he doesn't receive the stipulated amount, she now senses the contempt in his look "What utter disgust at incapacity. It was almost as if he could have struck me! A few hundreds instead of thousands made Sandip furious and unable to control his sudden revulsion of feeling, he sprang up from his seat towards me. . . . I flashed a lightning glance towards Amulya—the colour had left the boy's face as at the stroke of a whip. Then with all my strength I thrust Sandip from me. As he reeled back his head struck the edge of the marble table and he dropped on the floor." (148)

Her life now exhausted, Bimala has Amulya, she does not need Sandip to recognize the potential of her womanhood: "She sobbed and sobbed with deep feelings as Amulya touched Bimala's feet, 'This reverence of yours is the last touch of heaven left in my empty world'." (148) Tagore's understanding of the state of women in our society is so deep that he knew the fragile self of Bimala could still willingly yield to Sandip's influence. Sandip's adeptness in deception confuses Bimala as she admits "she loses power of seeing truth." (149) Sandip and Amulya's loud *Bande Mataram* captures her mind. She says: "I want to keep running to Sandip to hear him sing my praise." This alone could give substance to her vacuity. "I want to cleave to it night and day; for on whatever side I step among following there is only emptiness." (150) In states of vicissitudes, she suffers mercurial changes in her disposition from states of emptiness to state of explosive revelation and rage.

Sandip's jealousy with Amulya also is an eye opener to Bimala since she has "weaned him away from Sandip." (154) "That is why this sudden outburst of anger. He has understood that he cannot meet the power that I would, with mere strength. With a glance I can crumble his strongest fortification." (156) The ephemerality of emotions cannot be registered more tellingly when Bimala realizes that "the moment I had stolen my husband's money and paid it to Sandip, the music that was in our relation stopped. Not only did I destroy my own value by making myself cheap, but Sandip's powers, too lost scope for their full play." (156) Sandip had lost his aspect of the hero: "a tone of low quarrelsomeness has come into his words." (211) Amulya and Bimala together confess that the power and spell of Sandip has been broken. Bimala finds herself still at the threshold, the outside world is still not open to her. (172) Perhaps a fullest participation in the outside world could give her opportunity for expiation. Her hardest punishment is that she must put on Amulya the burden of her sin. (172)

Tagore's knowledge of the power of self-deception would not allow easy transformation in Sandip. He is still deceived, in the following chapter. (238) Bimala however is now capable of withholding herself from his control and sees through his rhetorics: "You had better go back and look up, your book, Sandip Babu. You are getting your words all wrong that's just the trouble with you trying to repeat this by rote." (175) Atin in Tagore's *Four Chapters* is also described in his own words as "word ridden." In this duel with Bimala, "Sandip the wielder of magic spell is reduced to utter powerlessness" from a king to the level of a boor." (176) But the drama of passion and repulsion will not end in simple gestures. In his final parting, Sandip sheds off the facade of hypocrisy in front of Nikhil; in this revelation, we discover some real moments of intense feelings and the depth of his passion for Bimala:

> "None but you, Queen Bee," he said, "will understand my words. . . . I salute you. With worship in my heart I leave you. My watchword has changed since you have come across my vision. It is no longer *Bande Mataram* (Hail Mother), but Hail Beloved, Hail Enchantress, the mother protects, the mistress leads to destruction . . . but secret is that destruction. You've made . . ." (177)

In rendering the protean nature of human responses and reactions, Tagore makes his Sandip a very authentic character. It is the feminity, the female power to which Tagore/Sandip is addressing—first pure revelation of Sandip. (244) Bimala sees the beauty in his demonic passion that was a lot more genuine than the histrionics of a stage hero of melodrama.

Bimala's muddled up revelations bring the novel's disarray to a serene linear pattern of knowledge. With heavy heart and the knowledge that the knowledge of life could give so much exhaustion, she muses: "I feel I want to die. Yet in my heart everything still lives—not even in death can I see the end of it all. Rather in death there seems to be even so much more of reopening what is to be ended should be ended in this life—there is no other way out." (185)

Nikhil and Bimala come to different levels of understanding and yet a more authentic mutual understanding. They have to come together to face the tragic fate awaiting them as a rebound of the riotous atmosphere of jingoism. The alienation of Muslim from the mainstream politics and the repercussion of Swadeshi at this juncture led to Muslim antipathy to Hindu sentiments and the events of cow-killing increase. Nikhil is maintaining an honesty of judgement in this regard. He observes: "*Shaktas* go on with their animal sacrifices just the same. They cannot be helped. We must let Mussalmans do as they think best. . . . If cow alone is to be held sacred, saved from slaughter, and not the buffalo, then that is bigotry, not religion." (162)

Nikhil's not joining the fanatic, sectarian sentiments make him unpopular, his effigy was burnt with enthusiasm and ceremony and other insults were hurled upon him. His sub-treasury is looted, an armed band raided the treasury and wounded Kasim, the man on the guard. The curious point was that they had taken only Rs. 6000/ and the rest was scattered on the ground: "The rest was out of question." Bimala knows the secret that it was Amulya who had stolen this amount to save the honour of his sister/mother, Bimala. As a consequence of the tension Kasim is made a suspect. Nikhil's honest sense of justice nonetheless would not allow him to make a case against his rival Harish Kundu either. The circumstances and their vicissitudes in the novel vindicate the position of Nikhil—his deep convictions prove their worth and relevance. Every action of violence and wrong inexorably has to have a rebound, be in violence of words or action. In Nikhil's character, Tagore's view of *Vasudhaiva Kutumbakam* as the political ideal appears forcefully. Tagore puts it in Nikhil's master Chandranath Babu's words:

> I tell you Nikhil, man's history has to be built by the united effort of all the races in the world, and therefore this getting of conscience for political reasons—this making a fetish of one's own country, won't do. (166)

Bimala now coming to terms with the sober truths of her situations attains maturity and a greater awareness of her true priorities. Sandip, repentant, returns the jewel box. Chandranath Babu announces the news of the rioting Mussalmans, and Nikhil and Amulya get killed.

Tagore's artistic freedom thus is sacrosanct that volitionally follows the dictates of this heritage: he fractures the hegemony of received modernity to connect us with our lost or misplaced secret and sacred selves. Reading his work today may help us recover and revitalize our cultural, intellectual and spiritual traditions. We may argue with his methods or conclusions, but shall have to concede that the central concern of his novel, *The Home and the World*, is *Purushartha*: *Dharma, Artha, Kama* and *Moksha.* His vision could certainly help us evolve a world view different from the dominant world view that the Western novel conveys. In trying to bring into harmony the ideas of the East and the West, he broadened the basis of Indian nationalism or rather evolved his version of ideal nationalism in consonance with Indian dharmic objectives and he hoped that "accordingly the next civilization will be based not merely upon economic and political competition and exploitation but upon worldwide social cooperation; upon spiritual ideals of reciprocity, and not upon economical ideals of efficiency. And then women will have their true place."[11] It was Tagore's immense service to India, as it has been Gandhi's in a different place, that he forced people out of the narrow grooves of thought and made them think of broader issues affecting humanity. The Indian version of humanism that is propounded in the novel, *The Home and the World* demonstrates Tagore's growth into an able spokesperson of India not only of her religious past but more of her present.

NOTES

1. Rabindranath Tagore, *The Home and the World* (1915; New Delhi: Penguin, 1985).
2. Rabindranath Tagore, *Gitanjali* (London: Macmillan, 1949), poem XXVII.
3. Rabindranath Tagore, *Personality* (New Delhi: Macmillan, 1985), p. 65.
4. Badrinath Chaturvedi, *Dharma, India and the World Order: Twenty One Essays* (Edinburgh: St. Press, 1993), p. 122.
5. Shibani Kinker Chaubey, *Colonialism, Freedom Struggle and Nationalism in India* (New Delhi: Bookland, 1995), p. 114.

6. *Personality*, p. 68.
7. Henry James, *Wings of Dove* (O.U.P 1984), p. 8.
8. *Personality*, p. 98.
9. William Radice, "Tagore's Poetic Power" in *Rabindranath Tagore: A Celebration of his Life and Work,* Rabindranath Tagore Festival 1986 (London: Precision Press, 1986), p. 111.
10. Dutta and Robinson, *Rabindranath Tagore: An Anthology* (London: Picador, 1997).
11. *Personality*, p. 65.

Nationalism under Scrutiny: *The Home and the World*

RAHUL SAPRA

As I write, the Nation celebrates its victory over Pakistan in the Kargil conflict: "We have given Pakistan a fitting reply," "What do the Pakistanis think India is?," "After all the Indian army is one of the best in the whole world," "I am proud to be an Indian"—Hail Nationalism! Almost eighty years have passed since Tagore lectured on the dangers of nationalism, perhaps in vain. Nationalism today is an even more potent ideological weapon than it was in the 1920s. However this is not to imply that Tagore was not patriotic; he was against the western form of nationalism, with its "iron chains of organization—the most relentless and unbreakable that have ever been manufactured in the whole history of man." (*Nationalism* 61) In *Nationalism* he observes that the essential difference between the British Empire and the Mughals and Pathans who invaded India is that "we had known them as human races—we had never known them as a nation," but in the case of the British Empire "we had to deal, not with kings, not with human races, but with a nation—we, who are no nation ourselves." (51) The imposition of the western form of nationalism onto Indian culture is subtly dealt with in his novel *The Home and the World* (1919).

The three narrators—Bimala, Nikhil and Sandip—are used to highlight contradictory aspects of nationalism. Nikhil comes closest to articulating Tagore's views on the subject, while Sandip who, in the novel, stands for Western nationalism takes the opposite stance. Bimala is caught between the two poles:

she is Nikhil's devout wife until she is taken in by Sandip's fiery brand of nationalism. The tension generated by the triangle of Bimala, Nikhil and Sandip exposes not only the dangers inherent in the western form of nationalism, but also, more importantly, the dangers in shaping the Indian 'nation' on the lines of Western nationalism.

Sandip's brand of nationalism is a direct product of the rise of positive science and naturalistic philosophy in the West, which reduced man to purely naturalistic terms and denied his metaphysical dimension. Man was conceived as a "natural being, subject to principle of profit and rational egoism: his metaphysical depth was taken away from him, his third dimension—the image of God." (Mochulsky, xxii) Therefore for Sandip the only relationship between man and the outer world is one of a constant struggle; a relationship based on a power equation:

> The lesson of the whole world is: 'That is really mine which I can snatch away.' My country does not become mine simply because it is the country of my birth. It becomes mine on the day when I am able to win it by force.

Every man has a natural right to possess, therefore greed is natural—what my mind covets, my surroundings must supply. This is the only true understanding between our inner and outer nature in this world. (49)

And in the process of accomplishing one's desires moral values are of no consequence: "Let moral ideals remain merely for those poor anaemic creatures of starved desire whose grasp is weak—Nature surrenders herself but only to the robber." (49) Moral precepts exist only for the ordinary:

> My [Sandip's] theory of life makes me certain that the Great is cruel. To be just is for ordinary men,—it is reserved for the great to be unjust. The surface of the earth was even. The volcano butted it with its fiery horn and found its own eminence,—its justice was not towards

> its obstacle, but towards itself. Successful injustice and genuine cruelty have been the only forces by which individual or nation has become millionaire or monarch. (99)

In Sandip's speech, one can trace the essence of western thought beginning from Machiavelli's Prince to the twentieth century, as exhibited in the works of Friedrich Nietzsche and Fyodor Dostoevsky, the two great minds who captured the essence of the disintegration of western civilization, perhaps, better than anybody else. Nietzsche in *Beyond Good and Evil* (1886) observes that "A living thing seeks above all to discharge its strength—life itself is Will to Power," (395) and then goes on to argue that there has to be a different set of moral values for the "higher class of men": "That which serves the higher class of men for nourishment or refreshment, must be poison to an entirely different and lower order of human beings. The virtues of the common man would perhaps mean vice and weakness in a philosopher." (415) Dostoevsky both in *The Brothers Karamazov* (1880) and *Crime and Punishment* (1866) deals with the question of morality vis-a-vis the disintegration of Western civilization. Sandip's views on morality are reminiscent of Raskolnikoff's views on the subject in *Crime and Punishment*: "An extraordinary man has a right—not officially—but from and by his very individuality—to permit his conscience to overstep certain bounds, only so far as the realization of one of his ideas may require it." (193) Raskolnikoff anticipates Sandip's division of men into two categories:

> Nature divides men into two categories: the first, an inferior one, comprising ordinary men, the kind of material whose function it is to reproduce specimens like themselves; the other, a superior one, comprising men who have the gift or power to make a new word, thought, or deed felt. To the first belong, in a general way, conservatives, men for order, who live in a state of obedience and love—such men cannot help obeying, because it is their destiny, and such an act has nothing humiliating for them.

> The next class, however, consists exclusively of men who break the law, or strive, according to their capacity or power, to do so. Their crimes are naturally relative ones, and of varied gravity. Most of them insist upon destruction of what exists in the name of what ought to exist. And if, in the execution of their idea, they should be obliged to shed blood, step over corpses, they can conscientiously do both in the interest of their idea. (194)

Thus it becomes obvious that through the character of Sandip, Tagore voices the predicament of the West at the beginning of the century. Sandip's idea of a nation is a product of the ideas prevalent in the West at the turn of the century. The danger which Tagore foresees is the imposition of the western idea of a nation onto Indian culture. In his lectures on nationalism delivered in Japan and America he succinctly voices his opinion on the subject:

> This political civilisation which has sprung up from the soil of Europe and is overrunning the whole world, like some prolific weed, is based upon exclusiveness—before this political civilisation came to its power and opened its hungry jaws wide enough to gulp down great continents of the earth, we had wars, pillages, changes of monarchies and consequent miseries, but never such a sight of fearful and hopeless voracity, such wholesale feeding of nation upon nation, such huge machines for turning great portions of the earth into mince-meat, never such terrible jealousies with all their ugly teeth and claws ready for tearing open each other's vitals. This political civilisation is scientific, not human. (*Nationalism*, 24)

If Sandip's views match with those of Nietzsche, Nikhil's are those of Tagore himself. The above-quoted words find a parallel in Nikhil's conversation with Sandip: "In Europe people look at everything from the viewpoint of science. But man is neither mere physiology, nor biology, nor psychology, nor even sociology—Man is infinitely more than the natural science of himself." (73) Instead of succumbing to the ideology of nationalism, Nikhil desires to "plant something greater than Swadeshi." (173) By refusing to equate the country with God, he questions Sandip's kind of nationalism, which in the process of equating one's country with God necessarily sees the other countries as potential enemies. Nikhil overturns Sandip's theory of equating the country with God, by arguing if "God manifests Himself both in man and in his country" then it follows logically that "there should be no difference for you [Sandip] between man and man, and so between country and country." (37) Nikhil takes the argument one step further by arguing that "since God is manifested in us, our self has to be worshipped before all else; because natural instinct claims it." (34) Nikhil's objection to the theory of nationalism is similar to the one that Tagore expresses in *Nationalism* when he says that the country is not "greater than the ideals of humanity." (83)

What are Tagore's objections to nationalism? Tagore argues that there is an essential difference between the former governments and the modern governments based on the nation-state. He says that in the days of the previous governments there were certain things "extremely distasteful" to us, but the difference is that those governments since they were "not governments by the Nation, their texture was loosely woven, leaving big gaps through which our own life sent its threads and imposed its designs." (61) He goes on to explain the difference with the help of the following example:

> When we walk barefooted upon ground strewn with gravel, our feet come gradually to adjust themselves to the caprices of the inhospitable earth; while if the tiniest particle of the gravel finds its lodgement inside our shoes we can never forget and forgive its intrusion. And these shoes are the government by the Nation—it is tight, it regulates our steps with a closed-up system, within which our feet have only the slightest liberty to make their own adjustments. (61)

Thus no matter how backward the previous system of governance was, it promised enough space for man's humanity to blossom; enough adaptability for man to adjust with other men. The ramifications of nationalism, on the other hand, were already visible in India at the beginning of the century when Muslims by and large remained aloof from the general current of nationalism. Along with the divide and rule policy of the English, the separatist politics of some Muslim leaders, and the talk of Hindu Rashtra by some Hindu leaders led to the alienation of the Muslims. Both Nikhil and Sandip raise this issue in the novel. Nikhil observes: "If the idea of a United India is a true one—[then] Mussalmans are a necessary part of it"; (158) whereas Sandip's view is that "we shall never be able to bring them wholly round to our side. So they must be suppressed altogether and made to understand that we are the masters." (158) Partha Chatterjee in *The Nation and its Fragments: Colonial and Postcolonial Histories* (1994) argues that the failure of the Indian nation to effectively include within its body the whole of the demographic mass that it claims to represent becomes evident "when we note that the formation of a hegemonic 'national culture' was necessarily built upon the privileging of an 'essential tradition,' which in turn was defined by a system of exclusions. Ideals of freedom, equality, and cultural refinement went hand in hand with a set of dichotomies that systematically excluded from new life of the nation the vast masses of people whom the dominant elite would represent and lead, but who could never be culturally integrated with their leaders." (134)

Tagore further shows the contradictions within the Swadeshi movement. Nikhil's Master Chandranath Babu argues that the Swadeshi movement instead of making people independent is enslaving them. Nikhil tells the students, the followers of Sandip, that the imposition of Swadeshi is going to result in a loss for the "poor traders and their customers." (131) The fact that the people have to be forced, Nikhil tells the students, to follow the ideals of *Swadeshi* only goes on to show that the "whole country has not taken [the] vow." (133) Panchu's case shows that Swadeshi from one angle is nothing but the victimisation of poor traders by the zamindars. When Harish Kundu, the zamindar, insists upon burning the "foreign stuff" (135) that Panchu sells, Panchu makes an important remark: "I [Panchu] can't afford it! You [Harish Kundu] are rich; why not buy it and burn it?" (134) The fact that Harish Kundu does not do so and gives Panchu a beating only proves the Master's point that Swadeshi is nothing but a form of "Zamindars's oppression." (133) Even Bimala, no matter how passionately she is taken in by Sandip's idea of Swadeshi, always "felt ashamed of the inelegant, unfashionable furniture" (122) in Nikhil's reception-rooms, "especially when he had the magistrate, or any other European, as his guest." (122) She was afraid that the Europeans might take them for "barbarians, or at all events in wanting in refinements." (122) Therefore whenever she had news of "some European guest," (123) she would steal into her husband's room and replace the ordinary brass pot on his writing table with a "crystal vase of European make." (123)

However, she along with the majority of the people are taken in by Sandip's ideas for, unlike Nikhil's, the fire and passion which they generate not only make them far more tempting but also make them appear practical in effecting a change. But in the course of the novel it becomes obvious that it is Nikhil's views that are practical and not those of Sandip. Not only is Nikhil concerned about the poor traders but also takes pragmatic steps to let them survive the onslaught of Sandip's Swadeshi campaign. For instance, Nikhil buys Panchu's holdings to deter Harish Kundu from evicting Panchu for disobeying his orders banning the sale of foreign goods in the territory. It is not that Nikhil is totally against the ideals of Swadeshi, but he is able to see that a blind and impractical imposition of the ideals can ruin the poor traders. When Bimala asks him to let the traders sell Indian goods, Nikhil's reply is "nothing would please me better," (142) but what he objects to is that such a stance cannot be taken by the poor traders for they cannot afford it financially. And in such a situation if one goes ahead with the project of Swadeshi then it would not be short of "tyranny." (142) To

Bimala's objection: "It would not be tyranny for selfish gain," Nikhil replies, "To tyrannise for the country is to tyrannise over the country." (142) This is what Sandip and his followers refuse to acknowledge: the fact that India is a poor country which will make it difficult for the people to do full justice to the vow of Swadeshi that they have taken. Nikhil explains to Sandip and Bimala that the "excitement" and "drunkenness" generated by Swadeshi "may give strength, but not weapons." (117) Bimala's reply that "strength is the gift of God—Weapons can be supplied by mere mechanics" is undercut by Nikhil's realistic point of view: "The mechanic will claim wages before they deliver their supplies." (118) This is what Sandip lacks—a close knowledge of the ground reality. His exhortation: "Don't you [Nikhil] trouble about that. Their wages shall be paid" (118) later rebounds upon himself when to save his skin he forces Bimala to plunder her own house.

Sandip raises Bimala to the level of goddess Shakti but then degrades this goddess to the level of a petty thief. It is this that ultimately releases Bimala from the spell that he has cast upon her. By using Bimala for the cause of the country, Sandip not only makes Bimala feel that she is the country herself but at the same time imposes upon her the same values that he has inherited from the West: "I shall simply make Bimala one with my country. The turbulent west wind which has swept away the country's veil of conscience, will sweep away the veil of the wife from Bimala's face, and in that uncovering there will be no shame." (106) Sandip knows that to be able to exploit her the first step is to get her out of the confines of the home: "Are you for ever determined to make gods of your petty household duties,—you who have it in you to send us to life or to death?—Take your plunge today into the freedom of the outer world." (91-92) However he doesn't stop there. To completely 'liberate' her from the home he undermines the values that make a home. His offer to Bimala to work for the "Cause" (90) is also an invitation for an extramarital relationship: "let her gradually come to the conviction that to acknowledge and respect passion as the supreme reality, is to be modern,—not to be ashamed of it, not to glorify restraint. If she finds shelter in some such word as 'modern,' she will find strength." (74-75) He is to an extent successful in forcing his values upon Bimala, for she experiences a moment when, like Sandip, she feels "removed from the plane in which right and wrong, and the feelings of others, have to be considered." (119) It is under this spell of moral abnegation that she commits the theft. However the moment she commits the theft she experiences a reversal of values. Earlier Sandip had liberated her from the sense of right and wrong by making her one with the country, but now she equates the country with her home and feels responsible for the theft:

> I could not think of my house as separate from my country: I had robbed my house, I had robbed my country. For this sin my house had ceased to be mine, my country also was estranged from me. Had I died begging for my country, even unsuccessfully, that would have been worship, acceptable to the gods. But theft is never worship,—how then can I offer this gold? Ah me! I am doomed to death myself, must I desecrate my own country with my impious touch? (193)

Bimala's role can be better understood with regard to Partha Chatterjee's analysis of anticolonial nationalism. Chatterjee argues that the idea of nationalism in Asia and Africa is "posited not on an identity but rather on a difference with the 'modular' forms of national society propagated by the modern west." (5) The fundamental feature of anticolonial nationalism in Asia and Africa is that it separated the domain of culture into two spheres—the material and the spiritual:

> The material is the domain of the 'outside,' of the economy and of statecraft, of science and technology, a domain where the West has proved its superiority and the East has succumbed. In this domain, then, Western superiority had to be acknowledged and its accomplishments carefully studied and replicated. The spiritual, on the other hand, is an 'inner' domain bearing the 'essential'

> marks of cultural identity. The greater one's success in imitating Western skills in the material domain, therefore, the greater the need to preserve the distinctiveness of one's spiritual culture. (6)

He further observes that "the material domain, the nationalists argued, lies outside us—a mere external that influences us, conditions us, and forces us to adjust to it. Ultimately it is unimportant. The spiritual, which lies within, it is our true self; it is that which is genuinely essential." (120) Thus as long as India was able to retain the "spiritual distinctiveness of its culture, it could make all the compromises and adjustments necessary to adapt itself to the requirements of a modern material world without losing its true identity." (120) Tagore's views are almost similar to the above-stated formulation. While lecturing on the subject of nationalism in Japan he said that to the rigid structures of nationalism the East must apply its "eastern mind, spiritual strength, love of simplicity, recognition of social obligation in order to cut out a new path for this great unwieldy car of progress, shrieking out its loud discord as it ruins." (22) Thus retaining the spiritual essence in the onslaught of Western nationalism was for Tagore of the utmost importance. Applying the material/spiritual distinction to the matter of concrete day-to-day living, Chatterjee separates the social space into ghar and bahir, the home and the world:

> The world is the external, the domain of the material; the home represents one's inner spiritual self, one's true identity. The world is a treacherous terrain of the pursuit of material interests, where practical considerations reign supreme. It is also typically the domain of the male. The home in its essence must remain unaffected by the profane activities of the material world—and woman is its representation. (120)

Thus it becomes the responsibility of the women to retain the spiritual quality of the national culture. Tagore shows Bimala performing this function towards the end when she rejects the philosophy of Sandip, condemns herself for the theft, overcomes all desires for an extramarital relationship with Sandip and tries to save Amulya with her motherly love. Through Bimala's return to her home, Tagore appeals to the fellow Indians for a return to the spiritual values which India symbolizes. Instead of giving in to western nationalism, Indians should retain their spiritual identity and thereby find a solution not just for India but for the problem the whole world is facing. Tagore believes that the problem of India is the problem of world in miniature. India "is many countries packed into one geographical receptacle. It is just the opposite of what Europe truly is: namely, one country made into many." (88) According to him the problem of race unity, the basis of the ideology of nationalism, is the problem which the whole world is facing. Whereas India had always contained many races and "acknowledged the differences between them where these exist, and yet seek for some basis of unity" (78):

> What India has been, the whole world is now. The whole world is becoming one through scientific facility. And the moment is arriving when you must also find a basis of unity which is not political. If India can offer to the world her solution, it will be a contribution to humanity. There is only one history—the history of man. All histories are merely chapters in the larger one. And we are content in India to suffer for such a great cause. (78)

Thus instead of letting the world divide into numerous countries, Tagore raised his voice for a global order, but one based on a spiritual and not a political unity. With Nikhil, he believes that God manifests Himself both in man and his country "so there should be no difference between man and man and—between country and country." (37)

Works Cited

Chatterjee, Partha. *The Nation and its Fragments: Colonial and Post-colonial Histories* (Delhi: OUP, 1994).

Dostoevsky, Fyodor. *Crime and Punishment* (1866) (London: Penguin, 1997).

Mochulsky, Konstantin. Introduction, *The Brothers Karamazov*, trans. Andrew H. Macandrew (Toronto: Bantam, 1970).

Nietzsche, Friedrich. *Beyond Good and Evil: The Philosophy of Nietzsche* (New York: The Modern Library, 1954).

Tagore, Rabindranath. *The Home and the World* (1919), trans. Surendernath Tagore (Madras: Macmillan, 1992).

______, *Nationalism* (1917) (Delhi: Rupa, 1994).

The Conflict between Bondage and Liberation in *The Home and the World*

BASAVARAJ NAIKAR

The conflict between bondage and liberation happens to be the major thematic concern in Rabindranath Tagore's *The Home and the World*. The political theme of Indian nationalism, especially the Swadeshi movement and the emotional theme of man-woman relationship are intertwined beautifully in the novel. The interplay of these two themes is foregrounded in Bimala, the central character in the novel.

Although the novel is written from three points of view of Bimala, Nikhil and Sandip Babu, Bimala is 'the focal character reacting to two contradictory personalities. The novel is set in the early decades of the twentieth century Bengal which was marked by a political awakening and assertion of new national identity. The Indians, in the present case, the Bengalis, wanted to rebel against the British rule in the form of Swadeshi movement and rebellion against the British goods. But the rebellious Swadeshi movement was not a homogeneous one due to the contradictory interests and motives of people in the multi-cultural society of India. The Swadeshi movement was basically elitist in nature consisting of mainly the upper class and upper caste Bengalis who wanted to oppose the foreign goods on political grounds. But there was also a group of people especially from the poorer classes and castes who opposed it on economic grounds. The Swadeshi movement cost them their jobs and wages and led them to the brink of starvation. In the face of the existential problem of survival, the political opposition to the foreign goods appeared very impractical and destructive of the very means of their livelihood. Thus within the Indian, especially Bengali context, a rebellious movement was nullified by a counter-movement. The two contradictory schools of thought are clearly represented by Sandip Babu and Nikhil acting as binary opposites.

Whereas Nikhil is an idealist and rationalist who is not sympathetic to the Swadeshi movement, Sandip Babu is a fiery patriot who opposes the foreign rule very vehemently. Although Nikhil is a patriot, he sees the inadequacies and inconveniences caused by the Swadeshi movement. Being a landlord, he knows the economic tragedy that would be caused by the political rebellion against the foreign goods and cloths. But Sandip provides a sharp contrast to Nikhil who is a fiery revolutionary, an unscrupulous pragmatist and an opportunist.

Bimala who has married Nikhil wants to be a model of an ideal wife. Her illusion about the physical beauty of her husband as well as of herself is dispelled by the acceptance of reality. Neither her husband nor she has the physical beauty to be found in the fairyland. Soon after the marriage, her desire for physical beauty is transformed into an experience of spiritual beauty and consequently her disappointment about the lack of physical beauty is suppressed. Bimala develops a devotional attitude towards her husband who, in spite of his fabulous wealth, is known for his virtuous way of life like non-drinking and abstinence: "At that time the Prince of the fairy tale had faded, like the moon in the morning light. I had the Prince of my real world enthroned in my heart. I was his queen." (19) Thus Bimala's love for her husband is combined with a sense of reverence. The pious relationship between Bimala and Nikhil is summarized in the religious metaphor of the worship of the god by the devotee. Bimala discovers the beauty of devotion which is intangible and invisible. She deems herself lucky to enter the house of fortune and feels proud of having a 'stainless' husband. Soon she adjusts herself to the ways and customs as well as members of the royal family. The husband's home, thus, becomes a paradisal place for Bimala who is full of youthful desires and tender feelings. For her, her home is the whole world.

But Nikhil feels that his wife, who is highly sensitive, educated and cultured, should not be confined to the household life which is very limited and turns out to be almost a prison. He, therefore, suggests to her to extend her vision from home to the wide world: "I would have you come into the heart of the outer world and meet reality. Merely going on with your household duties, living all your life in the world of household connections and the drudgery of household tasks—you were not made for that! If we meet, and recognize each other, in the real world, then only will our love be true!" (23) Nikhil, thus, wants to liberate Bimala from the bondage of domestic life into the wide world outside, even when she is not aware of her bondage. He understands his wife better than she understands herself. He feels that his wife is like a "caged bird." His intense love for her impels him to see her enjoy life in its wider aspect. His catholicity of approach is expressed by him in the marine image: "The greedy man who is fond of his fish stew has no compunction in cutting up the fish according to his need. But the man who loves the fish wants to enjoy it in the water; and if that is impossible he waits on the bank, and even if he comes back home without a sight of it he has the consolation of knowing that the fish is all right. Perfect gain is the best of all; but if that is impossible, the next best gain is perfect losing." (24) Nikhil is, thus, a broadminded husband who wants to give full liberty to his wife to see or experience the wide world. In the context of Nikhil's home with all the vestiges of royal life, his willingness to extend freedom to his wife without her asking for it easily testifies to his magnanimity and belief in woman's emancipation in the first and second decades of the twentieth century Bengal.

The theme of woman's liberation is intertwined with that of political liberation of India. The Swadeshi movement which had started gathering momentum at this juncture was a preparatory stage in the nationalistic movement demanding the liberation of the country from the British rule. Sandip Babu is an ardent and enthusiastic leader of the Swadeshi movement, which brings a new excitement to the life of Bengalis at this time. *Bande Mataram* becomes a keyword of the movement. The patriots of Bengal hold meetings at different places of the land to mobilize the public opinion in their favour. People are thrilled by the new ideology of nationalism. Bimala's description of the meeting bears it out amply: "There is to be a big meeting in our temple pavilion. We women are sitting there, on one side, behind a screen. Triumphant shouts of *Bande Mataram* come nearer and to them I am thrilling through and through. Suddenly a stream of barefooted youths in turbans, clad in ascetic ochre, rushes into the quadrangle, like a silt-reddened freshet into a dry river-bed at the first burst of the rains. The whole place is filled with an immense crowd, through which Sandip Babu is borne, seated in a big chair hoisted on the shoulder of ten or twelve of the youths. *Bande Mataram! Bande Mataram! Bande Mataram!:* It seems as though the skies would be rent and scattered into a thousand fragments." (30)

Thus the political movement brings about a flood of enthusiasm in the hearts of men and women of Bengal. Bimala who is exposed to the public atmosphere of patriotism forgets her individual identity and identifies herself with the entire womanhood of the country: "I was utterly unconscious of myself. I was no longer the lady of the Rajah's house, but the sole representative of Bengal's womanhood. And he was the champion of Bengal. As the sky had shed its light over him, so he must receive the consecration of a woman's benediction." (31) Bimala, thus, comes under the powerful charismatic influence of Sandip Babu. She, therefore, invites him to dinner and attends on him soulfully. She considers herself as the *Shakti* of womanhood and is overwhelmed with admiration for his loquacity and patriotism. She falls in love with him without realizing it initially.

The arrival of Sandip Babu in Bimala's life enables her to understand her husband, Nikhil, from a contrastive perspective. Whereas Nikhil is a self-controlled, rational and idealistic man, Sandip Babu happens to be an impulsive, unscrupulous and practical man. Bimala seems to like Sandip Babu's boisterous life better than Nikhil's quiet life. Nikhil, who is a subtle psychologist endowed with a liberal approach to life, tries to understand the mind of his wife: "Her love is for the boisterous. From the tip of her tongue to the pit of her stomach she must tingle with red pepper in order to enjoy the simple fare of life. But my determination was, never to do my duty with frantic impetuosity, helped on by the fiery liquor of excitement. I know Bimala finds it difficult to respect me for this, taking my scruples for feebleness—and she is quite angry with me because I am not running amuck crying *Bande Mataram*." (42)

Just as Nikhil understands the nature of his wife, he understands the nature of Sandip also. He knows that Sandip hides his selfish desires under the guise of patriotism and religious rationalization: "I have been noticing for some time that there is a gross cupidity about Sandip. His fleshy feelings make him harbour delusions about his patriotism. His intellect is keen, but his nature is coarse, and so he glorifies his selfish lusts under high-sounding names. The cheap consolations of hatred are as urgently necessary for him as the satisfaction of his appetites. Bimala has often warned me, in the old days, of his hankering after money. . . . It will, however, be difficult to explain to Bimala today that Sandip's love of country is but a different phase of his covetous self-love. Bimala's hero-worship of Sandip makes me hesitate all the more to talk to her about him, lest some touch of jealousy may lead me unwittingly into exaggeration." (43)

Bimala's love for Sandip is intensified by his flattery. Sandip wants to have a source of inspiration for his nationalistic activities and therefore tries to consider Bimala as an embodiment of the whole nation: "I have never yet found any one source of inspiration suffice me for good. That is why I have been constantly moving about, rousing enthusiasm in the people, from which in turn I draw my own store of energy. Today you have given me the message of my country. Such fire I have never beheld in any man. I shall be able to spread the fire of enthusiasm in any country by borrowing it from you. No, do not be ashamed. You are far above all modesty and diffidence. You are the Queen Bee of our hive, and we the workers shall rally around you. You shall be our centre, our inspiration." (44) Bimala's ego is easily bloated by such flattery and consequently she feels proud of herself for being an incarnation of *Shakti* and of the nation. She decides to dedicate herself to the country's cause. Thus her personal love for Sandip and her political love for the nation are intertwined in a very subtle fashion, which is borne out by her words: "So long I have been like a small river at the border of a village. My rhythm and my language were different from what they are now. But the tide came up from the sea, and my breast heaved; my banks gave way and the great drumbeats of the sea waves echoed in my mad current. . . . Sandip's hungry eyes burnt like the lamps of worship before my shrine. . . . For Sandip Babu was not a mere individual. In him was the confluence of millions of minds of the country. When he called me the Queen Bee of the hive, I was acclaimed with a chorus of praise by all our patriot workers." (50)

Like Bimala, Sandip also feels drawn towards her: "The little red ribbon, which peeps through the luxuriant masses of her hair, with its flush of secret longing, it is the lolling tongue of the red storm cloud. I feel the warmth of each turn of her *sari*, each suggestion of her raiment, of which even the wearer may not be fully conscious." (55) Thus both Bimala and Sandip are mutually attracted to each other. Just as Sandip sees a sublimated image of India in her, she is overwhelmed by his poetic and patriotic language and thinks him to be a spokesman of all the patriots of India.

As Bimala's love for Sandip grows more and more intense, she begins to look at her husband from a rather negative perspective. Although she knows that her infatuation for Sandip is morally wrong, she is helplessly caught in the whirlpool of emotion: "For two whole days I did not stir out. Then, for the first time, I discovered how far I had travelled. My life felt utterly tasteless. Whatever I touched I wanted to thrust away. I felt myself waiting—from the crown of my head to the tips of my toes—waiting for something, somebody; my blood kept tingling with some expectation." (70) She begins to long for somebody other than her husband who cannot thrill her in spite of being good to her.

Nikhil, who is a subtle psychologist, has observed that his wife will, perhaps, be happier in the company of a man like Sandip than his own company. He, therefore, thinks of giving Bimala the freedom to choose the man of her choice and make her happy. He feels that keeping her under his thumb would be tantamount to enslavement or imprisonment. He had wanted Bimala to be an angel, but she has turned out to be an ordinary being of flesh and blood with all the human desires and weaknesses. Far from feeling jealous or angry with his wife, Nikhil wants to give her the liberty of accepting Sandip as her life-partner: "I must acknowledge that I have merely been an accident in Bimala's life. Her nature, perhaps, can only find the true union with one like Sandip." (65)

As days go by, Sandip grows more and more fascinated by Bimala as he sees her as an embodiment of the country: "Do you not know that I came to worship? Have I not told you that, in you, I visualize the *Shakti* of our country? The geography of a country is not the whole truth. No one can give up his life for a map! When I see you before me, then only do I realize how lovely my country is." (73) When Bimala hears the fiery speech of Sandip, she is not sure whether it is the fire of worship, or of passion. The growing intimacy between the two is tolerated by the large-hearted Nikhil, but not approved by the old-fashioned Bara Rani, sister-in-law of Nikhil.

There is a basic temperamental difference between Nikhil and Sandip. Sandip is aware of his own nature made of many contradictions. He knows that he is cruel and tender at the same time. But Nikhil is tender-hearted by and large. Whereas Sandip believes in success, Nikhil believes in Truth. Sandip wants to combine religion with nationalism, whereas Nikhil wants to keep them apart. Says Sandip: "We must have our religion and also our nationalism; our *Bhagvadgita* and also our *Bande Mataram*." (80) He tries to rationalize his love for Bimala as legitimate one and has no feeling of guilt or shame. "Why am I allowing my life to become entangled with Bimala's? . . . It is only too clear how she wants me, and so I look on her as quite legitimately mine. The fruit hangs on the branch by the stem, but that is no reason why the claim of the stem should be eternal. Ripe fruit cannot forever swear by its slackening stem-hold. All its sweetness has been accumulated for me; to surrender itself to my hand is the reason of its existence, its very nature, its true morality. So I must pluck it, for it becomes me not to make it futile." (81) Thus Sandip is bothered not about the means but only about the ends. For him religion becomes part of nationalism rather than vice versa. Likewise, even extra-marital love for Bimala is also part of his nationalistic programme. Thus he remains a practical and opportunistic revolutionary for whom everything is fair in the nationalistic war.

Nikhil, who has noticed the growing intimacy between Bimala and Sandip, wants to liberate his wife from bondage so that he can himself feel liberated: "This cry of pain must be silenced in me. So long as I continue to suffer, Bimala will never have true freedom. I *must* free her completely, otherwise I shall never gain *my* freedom from untruth." (86) Like his decision to liberate Bimala from the domestic bondage, he also takes a decision to liberate the country by removing the real cause of the country's sorrow *a la* Siddhartha. But Nikhil's idea of liberation is more psychological or spiritual than political. He wants his wife Bimala to participate in the activities of the wide world and understand life from a wider perspective.

As the nationalistic activities gather speed in the country, the love between Bimala and Sandip also grows more and more intense. Thus the emotional attachment and the ideological attachment get reinforced by each other. Bimala who is a docile wife has now begun to take deep interest in the rationalistic struggle of Bengalis headed by Sandip Babu. She, therefore, asks her husband to prevent the sale of foreign goods from their market in Suksar. But Nikhil does not agree to that, because he rightly thinks that the Swadeshi movement is basically elitist in nature inspiring only the upper class and upper-caste people of Bengal. He explains to Bimala that the people of lower classes or castes like petty merchants, labourers, workers and Muslim traders will have to lose their livelihood on account of the Swadeshi movement and that these people will rebel strongly against the Swadeshi movement. Thus there is a tension between the Swadeshi movement and a counter movement against it. But Bimala is not convinced by her husband's argument as she is deeply influenced and inspired by Sandip Babu's revolutionary ideology. In turn, she also wants to be a source of *Shakti* for Sandip. Her emotional attachment for Sandip is supported by the Vaishnava philosophy (of the *Shakti* of Delight) and is pragmatically combined with the feeling of nationalism. She is impelled by Sandip's poetic recitation to elevate herself from the level of a mere woman to that of a Goddess of Energy: "Listening to his allegories, I had forgotten that I was plain and simple Bimala. I was *Shakti*; also an embodiment of Universal joy. Nothing could fetter me, nothing was impossible for me; whatever I touched would gain new life. The world around me was a fresh creation of mine; for behold, before my heart's response had touched it, there had not been this wealth of gold in the Autumn's sky! And this hero, this true servant of the country, this devotee of mine—this flaming intelligence, this burning energy, this shining genius—him also I was creating from moment to moment. Have I not seen how my presence pours fresh life into him time after time?" (98) Bimala thus decides to break the bondage of domestic restrictions and encourage the nationalistic activities of Sandip Babu by inspiring him emotionally. Because of her ardent admiration for Sandip Babu, she accepts his disciple, Amulya also for affectionate treatment. As the Swadeshi movement gathers speed in Bengal as also in India in general, the patriots begin to burn German, British and other foreign cloths and goods, drown the boats and rob the shops in the market. There is great political and social turmoil in the country.

Just as the Swadeshi movement grows more and more widespread in Bengal, the emotional attachment of Bimala for Sandip Babu also becomes more intense. One day at a moment of emotional intensity, Sandip Babu presses the hand of Bimala who does not snatch it away, because of her love for him. Sandip Babu feels that now there has been perfect attachment between the two hearts. He describes it through a musical metaphor: "When I pressed Bimala's hand my nerves rang music, like tuned up strings; but the symphony stopped short at the first movement." (111) Sandip Babu realizes that in spite of the perfect attunement between them, he has to overcome a few obstacles.

When Sandip Babu is sure that Bimala is in love with him as well as with his political ideology, he thinks that he has a powerful hold upon her and therefore wants to wield his power over her by demanding a sacrifice from her, in order to test the intensity of her love. So, one day he puts forth his demand for fifty thousand rupees required for the expenses of the Swadeshi movement. Bimala is shocked a bit by the mention of such a big sum. Then Sandip Babu tries to soften her sense of shock by saying that although he requires Rs. 50,000 in the long run, he requires only Rs. 5000 for immediate purposes. Bimala who takes it as a challenge to her status as a Rani, agrees to pay it at the earliest opportunity. He tells her: "It shall be my supreme legacy to the Nation. Ignorant men worship gods. I, Sandip, shall create them." (125)

As the relationship between Bimala and Sandip grows deeper, the ideological difference between Nikhil and Sandip grows more conspicuous. The young students of Calcutta University holding scholarships from Nikhil accuse him of suppressing the workers on his estate and of being antipathic to the Swadeshi movement. They also betray the influence of Sandip Babu on them. But Nikhil refuses to be affected by their talk. On the domestic side, he has already noticed the intimacy between Bimala and Sandip and the way Bimala has been secretly pining for her lover. He, therefore, wants to make her happy by granting her the liberty she so badly wants. He tells her openly: "Why should I seek to keep you fast in this closed cage of mine? Do I not know that thus you cannot but pine and droop? . . . I know that if I insist on keeping you shackled my whole life will be reduced to nothing but an iron chain. What pleasure can that be to me? . . . So I tell you, truly, Bimala, you are free. Whatever I may or may not have been to you, I refuse to be your fetters." (134)

Now that Nikhil has granted freedom to his wife, he feels free. His introspection amply testifies to it: "I had simply come to understand that never would I be free until I could set free. To try to keep Bimala as a garland round my neck, would have meant keeping a weight hanging over my heart. . . . To clutch hold of that which is untrue as though it were true, is only to throttle oneself. May I be saved from such self-destruction." (134) Now that Bimala is liberated from the domestic, hence matrimonial restrictions, she begins to think of the meaning of freedom. Although she had felt that her idealistic husband had been so intangible like a dream, his grant of freedom to her seems to have resulted in his withdrawal of loving affection. She feels that her freedom is nothing but empty and meaningless: "And then, the other day in the garden, how easy my husband found it to tell me that he set me free. But can freedom—empty freedom—be given and taken so easily as all that? It is like setting a fish free in the sky—for how can I move or live outside the atmosphere of loving care which has always sustained me?" (137) Bimala, thus, realizes the emptiness of her freedom granted by her husband. But even then, it helps her indirectly to hobnob with Sandip Babu, with greater abandon. She feels irresistible pangs of separation from Sandip and grows impatiently mad to meet him. As she confesses: "The very next day I saw Sandip; and madness, naked and rampant, danced upon my heart. What was this? Was this, then my truer self? Never. I had never before known this shameless, this cruel one within me. The snake-charmer had come, pretending to draw this snake from within the fold of my garment—but it was never there, it was his all the time. Some demon had gained passion of me, and what I am doing today is the play of his activity—it has nothing to do with me." (141) Bimala is, thus, totally possessed by the object of her love combining in itself the amorous with the patriotic dimensions.

Since Bimala has decided to help Sandip Babu in his Swadeshi movement, she wants to give him the required amount of 5000 rupees. But she does not know how to arrange for the said amount. Nor does she wish to request her husband for money. She, therefore, steals twenty rolls of gold, in spite of the feeling of guilt and fear about it. When Sandip asks for the money for the second time as if with some authority over her, she gives him gold. Sandip is so grateful to her that he rushes towards her for bowing down to her feet. But Bimala thinks that he is trying to harm or molest her, and pushes him away forcefully. For a moment she feels confused about Sandip's behaviour. She introverts about him: "There must be two different persons inside men. One of these in me can understand that Sandip is trying to delude me, the other is content to be deluded. Sandip has power, but no strength of righteousness. The weapon of his which rouses up life smites it again to death. He has the unfailing quiver of the gods, but the shafts in them are of demons." (149)

Bimala thus cannot understand the true nature of Sandip in spite of his charismatic effect upon her. But Sandip surprises her by bowing down to her and clarifying his motive: "Goddess, it was to offer my reverence that I had approached you, but you repulsed me, and rolled me in the dust. Be it so. I accept your repulse as your boon to me. I raise it to my head in salutation." (149) Again, Bimala is won over by his praise. She is aware of her radiant sin, but, she remains very helpless because of her weakness for flattery: "Praise, praise. I want unceasing praise. I cannot live if my wine-cup be left empty for a single moment. So, as the very price of my life, I want Sandip of all the world, today." (150)

As Bimala has realized her sinfulness of being in a league with her lover, she feels guilty to face her husband: "When my husband nowadays comes in for his meals I cannot sit before him; and yet it is such a shame not to be near him that I feel I cannot do that either. So I seat myself where we cannot look at each other's face." (150) But in spite of this feeling of guilt, Bimala continues to support the country's cause through Sandip's activities. Meanwhile Sandip tries to wield his power over her in a subtle fashion. When Bimala offers some gold to Amulya either to pawn or sell it and get Rs. 6000 without Sandip's knowledge about it, Sandip gets angry and begins to quarrel with her. Bimala begins to understand his crude and cheap nature disguised under the facade of poetic patriotism: "The moment I had stolen my husband's money and paid it to Sandip, the music that was in our relations stopped. Not only did I destroy all my own value by making myself cheap, but Sandip's powers too, lost scope for their full pay. You cannot employ your marksmanship against a thing which is right in your grasp. So Sandip has lost his aspect of the hero; a tone of low quarrlcsomeness has come into his words." (156) Bimala is, thus, disenchanted with Sandip at least partially.

While the Swadeshi movement is in its full swing, the counter-movement by the poorer sections of the society, especially the Muslims begins to gather tempo. Nikhil, who learns about the Muslims' intention of attacking Sandip and his group, warns Sandip about it well in advance and suggests that he should leave the estate and go to Calcutta. There is a blatant difference of opinion and exchange of words between Nikhil and Sandip. Nikhil also wants to leave for Calcutta. As expected, the Muslims indulge in occasional cow-killing and fanatical activities. But Nikhil, being a rationalist, does not see much difference between the cow-killing by Muslims and the buffalo-killing by Hindus. There is a great deal of turbulence in the society. The Chakua Sub-Treasury is looted and Kasim the guard is suspected to have a hand in that. Nikhil wants to take Bimala to Calcutta to give her a broad vision of life.

While the political unheaval persists in the country, Bimala enters into new difficulties in her secret dealings with Sandip. She begins to suffer from anxiety after sending Amulya to sell her gold and get the money. She worries that Amulya may not return safe or alive because of his innocence and the risky atmosphere in the country. But Sandip has created a new trouble for her. He has cleverly stolen the jewel-box from Amulya's trunk and hurls it back at Bimala, thereby shocking and mocking her all the more. Bimala is deeply disenchanted by her greed and high-handed behaviour. When Amulya returns with six thousand rupees, Bimala heaves a sigh of relief. But she learns from Amulya that he has got the money the wrong way and, therefore, admonishes him gently. She asks him to put back the money from where he took it. She expiates her sin of involving the innocent Amulya in the risky job of getting the money.

When Sandip meets her unwantedly and tries to impress her with book-learned discourses, Bimala insults him as she can see through his words and understand his basic weakness, cheapness and crudeness. This is a moment of her liberation from the illusion of love. She is totally disenchanted by Sandip who exhibits his egotism and megalomania under the guise of poetic patriotism: "Sandip, the wielder of magic spells, is reduced to utter powerlessness, whenever his spell refuses to work. From a king he fell to the level of a boor. Oh, the joy of witnessing his weakness! The harsher he became in his rudeness, the more did this joy well up within me. His snaky coils, with which he used to snare me, are exhausted—I am free. I am saved, saved. Be rude to me, insult me, for that shows you in your truth; but, spare me your songs of praise, which were false." (176)

Bimala is really puzzled by the contradictions in Sandip's personality. She has seen through his words and actions. In his words, she notices that she has changed her position from a mother to that of an enchantress leading him to destruction. Although the fire of life in him is true, yet he appears like the stage hero of a melodrama. On the whole he appears to be a mysterious figure to her. When forced by Nikhil to leave the estate for Calcutta, Sandip bids farewell to her in his usual poetic fashion: "Goddess, I also set you free today. My earthen temple could hold you no longer—every moment it was on the point of breaking apart. Today I depart to worship your larger image in a larger temple. I can gain you more truly only at a distance from yourself. Here I had only your favour, there I shall be vouchsafed your boon." (179) Thus both Bimala and Sandip are liberated from the bondage caused by temporary infatuation and enchantment. In a way, both of them have metaphorically traversed from a narrow vision to a broader vision; from confusion to clarity and from ignorance to knowledge.

After the departure of Sandip from the estate, Bimala suffers from loneliness and anxiety for Amulya's safety. In the political turbulence, things happen in a very unexpected manner. When the Police Sub-Inspector comes with arrested Amulya, Bimala is really shocked. When Nikhil asks Amulya why he is caught by the police, Amulya confesses his crime of stealing the money from the treasury by threatening the guard, Kasim, by firing the bullets in the air. He further reveals that all this daredevilry he did only to please the sister, Bimla Rani.

Bimala is happy about the safe return of Amulya, but is worried about the key missing from her husband's key-bunch. When the whole house is searched for the key, Bimala confesses that she has the key and that she has spent the whole money for pleasure. But Nikhil is such a large-hearted man that he does not utter a single word of complaint against Bimala. On the contrary, he blames himself for making her steal the money instead of demanding it from him. Bimala's respect for her husband increases because of his magnanimity. She, therefore, touches his feet with her head in obeisance. In a way, she feels liberated from the world of ephemeral passion and enters the eternal world of worship. Love is combined with worship in her attitude to her husband: "Now is the time to set sail towards that great confluence, where the river of love meets the sea of worship. In that pure blue all the weight of its muddiness sinks and disappears. I now fear nothing—neither myself, nor anybody else. I have passed through fire. What was inflammable has been burnt to ashes; what is left is deathless. I have dedicated myself to the feet of him, who has received all my sin into the depths of his own pain." (199) Nikhil metaphorically becomes a Nilakantha who swallows the poison and retains it in his throat.

The peaceful lull is followed by a disturbing storm of events. When Bimala is recomposing herself, Sandip returns unexpectedly and gives back her jewel-box to her. Pursued as he is by Muslims, he rushes away from there. Political turbulence has increased in Bengal. The Muslims have planned to loot Harish Kundu's treasury. Nikhil wants to go there. Even when dissuaded by Bara Rani and Bimala, he turns a deaf ear to them and rushes there along with Amulya. But alas, he never returns alive. At night Nikhil is brought in a palanquin. He is mortally wounded in the head. And Amulya is killed by a bullet in the heart. The lives of innocent Nikhil and Amulya are sacrificed in the anti-Swadeshi violence. The tragic deaths of Nikhil and Amulya are as undeserved as unexpected. Bimala is compelled to accept the tragedy of widowhood in the most ironical way. Nikhil who helps Sandip escape from the Muslim pursuers, gets killed by them whereas Sandip uses his practical wisdom to escape.

The Home and the World is thus an interesting novel depicting man-woman relationship against the political background of Swadeshi movement in Bengal in the early part of the twentieth century. One may easily see the theme of various kinds of bondage and liberation intersecting one another. Although the domestic and the political setting in the novel is realistic, the style of depiction is poetic and typically Tagorean. One can see the echoes of Tagore's poetry in this novel. The Western critics like George Lukacs, habituated to the novels of social realism, have not been able to appreciate this poetic novel properly. As rightly pointed out by Anita Desai, the style of the novel which is very poetic and philosophical at the same time is the natural consequence of the Indian mind expressing itself through the convoluted and poetic Bengali language. It is perhaps inevitable for a poet to write a poetic novel. Hard and fast rules of social realism of the Western mode need not be applied to an essentially Bengali novel. It is high time for Western critics to reorient themselves to read and enjoy typically Oriental, non-Western literature instead of underrating it from the strait-jacket Eurocentric theories of novel.

The Other Side of Nationalism in *The Home and the World*

NOVY KAPADIA

Rabindranath Tagore's consistent critique of the Swadeshi movement and terrorism in his novel *Ghare-Baire* or *The Home and the World* exposed the author to a barrage of criticism. Critical reaction to his novel, serialised in the Bengali journal *Sabujpatra* in 1915 was harsh and hostile. This attitude persisted for some decades after the novel was published. The harsh criticism of Tagore's novel *The Home and the World* was mainly due to the depiction of Sandip, the swadeshi extremist and college friend of Nikhilesh the zamindar of Shukshayar. Sandip is depicted as a firebrand activist who used populist rhetoric to impress and manipulate Bimla and young followers like Amulya with his ultra-nationalist sentiments. By such a depiction, Tagore raised several pertinent questions about the nature and justification of the swadeshi movement. Tagore is implying that the swadeshi movement was not yet a grassroots movement but the impetus was primarily urban and bourgeois. The swadeshi movement refers to the banning of foreign goods and the desire to create an image of the motherland in the mould of Hindu goddesses. Bankim Chandra Chatterjee in his *Anandamath* (1882) first suggested the latter idea. In the novel Nikhilesh and his teacher *Mastermoshai* reveal that swadeshi was not an all-embracing struggle involving the lower classes, lower castes and other religions but an urban movement imposed on poor traders and peasants often Muslims who could not afford the luxury of the political struggle. Swadeshi goods were more expensive and of inferior quality to foreign goods. Critics however construed that Tagore displayed a lack of patriotic feelings and did not uphold the cause of nationalism. It is only in the last decades of the twentieth century, when the phenomenon of the world as a global village has taken roots that critical reactions to *The Home and the World* have altered. Critics have now realised that Tagore viewed swadeshi in a historical perspective and not just as a nationalist cause.

To understand why critics felt that Tagore was not favouring the national cause, let us evaluate what is the meaning and significance of the term nationalism. The commonly accepted dictionary meaning of nationalism is a movement favoring independence for a country that is controlled by or forms part of another. The word also evokes patriotic feelings or principles or efforts. However let us try to understand nationalism in a political and historical perspective. Such an understanding will enable us to gauge the reactions to Tagore's novel, *The Home and the World* in a better light.

Nationalism, in modern history, is a movement in which the nation-state is regarded as paramount for the realization of social, economic, and cultural aspirations of a people. Nationalism is characterized principally by a feeling of community among a people, based on common descent, language, and religion. Before the eighteenth century, when nationalism emerged as a distinctive movement, states usually were based on religious or dynastic ties; citizens owed loyalty to their Church or ruling family. Concerned with clan, tribe, village, or province, people rarely extended their interests nationwide.

The beginnings of modern nationalism may be traced back to the disintegration, at the end of the Middle Ages, of the social order in Europe and of the cultural unity of the various European states. The cultural life of Europe was based on a common inheritance of ideas and attitudes transmitted in the West through Latin, the language of the educated classes. All Western Europeans adhered to a common religion, Catholic Christianity. The break-up of feudalism, the prevailing social and economic system, was accompanied by the development of larger communities, wider social interrelations, and dynasties that fostered feelings of nationality in order to win support for their rule.

Historically, various technological, cultural, political, and economic advances fostered the tendency toward nationalism. Improvement in communications extended the knowledge of people beyond their village or province. The spread of education in vernacular languages to the lower-income groups gave them the feeling of participation in a common cultural heritage. Through education, people learned of their common background and tradition and began to identify themselves with the historical continuity of the nation. The introduction of national constitutions and the struggle for political rights gave people the sense of helping to determine their fate as a nation and of sharing responsibility for the future well-being of that nation. At the same time, the growth of trade and industry laid the basis for economic units larger than the traditional cities or provinces.

Most modern nations have developed gradually on the basis of common ties of descent, religion, and language. Several exceptions exist, however, notably Switzerland, the United States, Israel, and India. Switzerland is a nation in which no common religion or language was ever established. The Swiss include many adherents to both the Roman Catholic and Protestant religions; they have no linguistic unity, for German, French, and Italian are spoken in distinct regions of the country. Swiss nationalism was fostered primarily by isolation in a mountain region, the determination to maintain political independence, and rivalry among imperial powers, which kept each from aggression against Switzerland.

The United States was formed largely by British immigrants with disparate religious ties and was developed to a great extent by other immigrants having little in common except a yearning for religious, economic, and political freedom. Although the United States is unilingual, American nationalism was based primarily on a dedication to the concept of individual liberty and representative government derived from British traditions. What was considered in Great Britain the birthright of Britons became in the United States, under the influence of eighteenth-century Enlightenment, the natural right of every person. The Declaration of Independence marked the consummation of this libertarian ethos.

Israel was formed almost entirely from the immigration of diverse national groups of Jews who shared a common ideal based on religious nationalism. The traditional aspirations of Jews for a national revival in Palestine had remained unfulfilled for almost 2,000 years. As a result of genocide perpetrated by the National Socialist rulers of Germany before and during World War II, Jewish national aspirations suddenly achieved dynamic force. More than a million refugees from many different countries immigrated to Palestine. They learned Hebrew, the re-created national language, and established a new state with Judaism as the state religion. Among world Jewry, however, the Jews of Israel are a minority; most Jews continue to live as minority religious groups in their native countries.

A commonly accepted view by political and social scientists is that India is a nation in which Hinduism served as the cohesive traditional element in uniting peoples of various races, religions, and languages. Tagore differed from such a traditional view of India. Tagore has often described India as a "seaboard of great humanity where hosts of people emanating from diverse places intermingled with a single body." (Mukhopadhyay 31) In his book on *Nationalism* (1917), Tagore says, "India has never had a real sense of nationalism." (83) Throughout his life, Tagore denounced religious bigotry, casteism and parochialism and dreaded nationalism as a potent ideological weapon. For him race unity is a very important binding force in a nation. In *Nationalism*, he articulates, "There is only one history—the history of man. All national histories are merely chapters in the larger one." (78) By such views Tagore anticipated the phenomenon of Globalism over eighty years ago.

India's only Nobel Laureate for Literature has always felt that real differences between races must be acknowledged but yet some basis for unity should be sought. Tagore felt that in Indian history there were several examples of saints who preached and practised the cause of race unity. "The basis (of unity) has come through our saints, like Nanak, Kabir, Chaitanya and others preaching one God to all races of India." (78) In fact Tagore has extolled India as a country "which seldom indulged in territorial expansion." (Mukhopadhyay 31) One of the major concerns in *The Home and the World* is that the author is concerned at the imposition of western nationalism on the Indian psyche. In *Nationalism* he observes the major contrast between the British Empire and the Mughals and Pathans who had invaded India in earlier centuries. Talking about the Mughals and Pathans he said: "we had known them as human races, with their own religions and customs, likes and dislikes—we had never known them as a nation." (51) However in the case of the British Empire, "we had to deal not with human races but with a nation—we who are no nation ourselves." (51) So Tagore rejects the notion popularised by Western historians that India achieved national unity through the influence of Western ideas, notably those of British origin, and in struggle against British rule. The famous poet-novelist of Bengal did not approve of the popular imperialist concept of the white man's burden of civilising the East (by East is meant Asians, the British Empire also colonised China, Malaysia or Malaya as it was known then, Burma, Singapore and parts of West Asia and the French and Dutch also had areas of influence). Instead, Tagore argued that the political ideology and administrative practices imposed by the British were not beneficial for India. He states, "When this organisation of politics and commerce whose other name is the Nation, becomes all powerful at the cost of the harmony of the higher social life, then it is an evil day for humanity." (53) Tagore warns that "this [Western imposed concept] nationalism is a cruel epidemic of evil that is sweeping over the human world of the present age and eating into its moral vitality." (56)

The author's concern about the contradictory aspects of nationalism get reflected in his *The Home and the World.* Nikhil the educated and liberal zamindar of Shuksayar articulates Tagore's views on the contentious issue of nationalism. In contrast his college friend Sandip, the fiery swadeshi expounds the western view of nationalism. Nikhil's spirited wife Bimala, whom he persuades to leave purdah is initially infatuated by Sandip's mesmeric personality, charismatic leadership and eloquence. The enchanted Bimala is manipulated to steal money from the family safe and hand it over to Sandip for the cause. So the book is a series of monologues and has multiple focalisations. By depicting Sandip's mesmeric hold over his followers and Bimala, Tagore is warning against the dangers of rhetoric. The author implicitly hints at the hazards of the western notions of nationalism through the inherent tension caused by this trio of characters, Nikhilesh, Sandip and Bimala. In the novel there is an intermingling of the personal and political themes. Tagore poses a number of queries in the novel, about the nature and justification of the swadeshi movement, gender roles and the nature of reality and freedom. Through the subtle nuances of the debates and inner thinking of the characters, Tagore warns of the dangers of the ideology of nationalism imported from the west, masquerading as swadeshi and the inherent Indian tradition of tolerance and peaceful coexistence.

Tagore's views on the dangers of jingoism were quite clairvoyant. Many years later, the noted Marxist scholar Randhir Singh, a retired professor of Political Theory of the University of Delhi, explained how nationalism was like a double-edged sword. It could serve as a liberationist force as well as a means of domination. Randhir Singh was invited to deliver a lecture on "Nation and Nationalism" on Premchand's birth centenary on July 31, 1999 at a meeting convened by the progressive Hindi periodical *Hans*. In the course of his lecture, he said: "Located as we are in the Third World and with the still-alive, though rapidly fading memories of the long struggle against imperialism, we in this country are conventionally inclined to see nationalism as a liberationist force or ideology. But we will do well to remember that during the same period ruling classes of the countries of imperialism were finding nationalism useful not only to consolidate their rule at home but also to defend and justify their aggression and domination abroad." (29)

Randhir Singh revealed instances in recent history of political ideological use of nationalism by ruling class politicians. He cites the instance of Margaret Thatcher of England who evoked cries of nationalism and former glory during the Falklands war to rout her rivals the Labour Party in the elections during the 1980s.

In India, Randhir Singh commented on how Rajiv Gandhi romped home in an unprecedented electoral triumph of 1984 on a platform of nationalism with strong Hindu chauvinist, even anti-Sikh, overtones. Randhir Singh termed this development as "the emerging platform of Hinduised Indian nationalism, which has now been well and properly appropriated by another political formation of the ruling classes, the Bharatiya Janta Party." (29) The political scientist Randhir Singh conveys in his lecture what Tagore was indicating in the novel, that a nationalist perspective does not in itself mean an end to oppressive socio-economic structures or contradictions within society. Randhir Singh clarifies: "Thus understood in historical terms, nationalism is not in itself progressive or reactionary, secular or communal, democratic or authoritarian, anything better or worse. It all depends upon its specific character, its programme and leadership and above all, concrete historical context and conjecture." (29)

However before proceeding further it must be pointed out that nationalism played a pivotal role in the anti-colonial movements of the early twentieth century. Renowned critic Aijaz Ahmed shows that most anti-colonial movements, even those that became socialist and communist with a mass base, started as nationalist movements. In his perceptive essay, "A Century of Revolutions," Aijaz writes: "If all the socialist revolutions of Asia and Africa took the form of national liberation movements, it was also the case that all the communist and socialist movements in our continents which became mass movements did so in the perspective and environment of nationalism."

Aijaz however draws a distinction between revolutionary nationalism and national movements inspired by the bourgeois such as the Swadeshi agitation referred to by Rabindranath Tagore in his novel. Aijaz draws a distinction between revolutionary nationalism and ethnic nationalism. He explains: "a revolutionary nationalism, it thought of nationalism not as something that closes in upon itself and excludes others, as ethnic nationalisms of today do, but as part of an international movement against the common colonial enemy. Thus socialism had a deeply civilising influence upon nationalism itself, rescuing it from chauvinism and bigotry, and giving it a universalist content." (124)

Aijaz supports this view with examples from history. He says that a wide variety of leaders around the world ranging from Nelson Mandela to Yasser Arafat who were by no means communists themselves refused to become part of anticommunist crusades. He also showed that many radical nationalist regimes, from Nasser's Egypt to FLN's Algeria, which suppressed communism within their own country, nevertheless carried out reforms inspired by socialism and relied a lot on the erstwhile USSR in their struggles for independence from imperialism. Aijaz even suggests that the non-alignment movement stemmed from feelings of radical nationalism and survived because of the support of socialist countries. The authors of the non-aligned movement were Zhou En-lai of China, Prime Minister Jawaharlal Nehru of India, President of Egypt Gamal Abdel Nasser, President Sukarno of Indonesia and Marshal Tito of erstwhile Yugoslavia.

The concept of the non-aligned movement first emerged in the Bandung Conference of April 1955, attended by twenty-nine African and Asian nations. By 1961 it became an international movement which tried to maintain the balance of power in the prevailing Cold War between the two super powers USA and the erstwhile USSR. Aijaz feels that the fortunes of radical nationalism had a deep link with the socialist project. He feels that the collapse of the Soviet Union was as much a setback for anti-imperialist nationalisms as for the workers' movement. According to him, the spate of ethnic and religious nationalisms such as the Taliban movement in Afghanistan and the Serbian movement in the 1990s tend to be overwhelmingly right wing as they lack the inspiration from socialism.

Viewed in the context of Nationalism, *The Home and The World*, can thus be classified as Tagore's analysis of the swadeshi agitation. He felt it was not a revolutionary movement but an urban, middle class uprising which excluded the lower castes and poor classes of society. The downtrodden as victims are frequently mentioned in the novel. The author through the reflections of Nikhil suggests concern that the swadeshi movement claiming to be a nationalist cause had lost its moorings and had not succeeded in involving all sections of society. If we refer to Aijaz Ahmed's definitions it would imply that the swadeshi movement was not a radical nationalist movement. Anita Desai, in her introduction to the Penguin edition of the novel writes that Tagore was himself concerned that there was something basically wrong with the movement. He pitied the students who were hoodwinked into giving up their schools and colleges to become followers of dubious political leaders and gloating over bonfires of imported cloth. As Anita Desai explains, Tagore increasingly felt that the swadeshi agitation had become an elitist movement, run by the educated and landowning classes, the *bhadralok* of Bengal who had no connection and little sympathy for the labouring classes.

The author's major concern was that the cause had a class basis and had unwittingly led to a communal divide. He felt that the boycott of cheap British goods in favour of expensive and poorly made Indian goods was harming the interests of the poor people for whom swadeshi was merely an abstract and distant term. As a sensitive observer of social reality, he could also see that the sufferers were chiefly Muslim peasants and traders who became "resentful of wealthy Hindu landowners and politicians who could afford the luxury of idealism in the form of bonfires into which British goods were flung." (9) Tagore was also worried that instead of a syncretic civilisation, different communities (Hindus and Muslims) were becoming antagonistic to each other. Initially the Muslim peasants and small traders were sullen and did not cooperate in the swadeshi movement. Gradually the economic crises and suspicion fuelled an upsurge of protests and communal disturbances. As Anita Desai writes, "Tagore was horrified to find that the movement that had been conceived to fight the communalist forces set free by the British had itself become violently communal." (9) Tagore's disillusionment with the cause and his reply to his critics were embodied in his novel *The Home and the World.*

Several instances in this novel reveal the class bias of the votaries of the swadeshi movement. Panchu a poor trader is fined one hundred rupees by his zamindar Harish Kundu and threatened with eviction from the land. In desperation Panchu defiantly blurts out to Harish Kundu, "I can't afford it! You are rich; why not buy it up and burn it?" (104) The pleas of Panchu are ignored. An enraged Kundu gives him a shoe-beating instead and Panchu's purchased goods are burnt. This incident shows how the poor became victims of the zealous champions of the swadeshi movement. It also reveals the class character of this agitation. Most of the champions of swadeshi were landlords, impressionable students and officials or *babus* and neighbourhood hoodlums. Because of their class bias and zeal, these people had never thought of the suffering of the poor. This is indicated in the conference between the students, Nikhil and Mastermoshai during the holidays. The students protest to Nikhil and demand that he should banish foreign goods from the Suksar market. Nikhil and Mastermoshai try to reason with them. They explain that the nation is not just an abstraction but means the people living on the soil. Nikhil's master cautions the over-zealous students and says: "Have you wasted so much as a glance as to what was happening to them [men of the soil]? But now you would dictate what salt they shall eat, what clothes they shall wear. Why should they put up with such tyranny, and why should we let them?" (101)

So the master shows that the imposition of swadeshi is resulting in a loss for the traders and their poor customers. Nikhil also adds that he is concerned that people have to be forced to follow the ideals of swadeshi and the "whole country had not taken the vow." (102) However the students remain unmoved and make sarcastic remarks that Nikhil is worried about a decline in profits and so is not banning foreign goods. They depart from the meeting with chants of *Bande Mataram*. The debate between the idealistic students and the practical Nikilesh and his master foregrounds a perpetual argument about the conflict between political freedom and the desire for basic necessities.

Shashi Tharoor in his analytical book on *India from Independence to the Millennium* terms this as "The bread-versus-freedom-debate." He states that this is an important debate facing both India and the world at the end of the twentieth century. Tharoor writes, "Can democracy deliver the goods" to alleviate desperate poverty, or do its in-built inefficiencies only impede rapid growth? (3) The type of nationalism that has enamoured the students of Suksar is authoritarian. It is not the type of economic and cultural nationalism, which led to Kentucky Fried Chicken outlets being ransacked by irate mobs of farmers in Bangalore in the mid-1990s. Instead the students are inspired by an abstraction called nationalism and remain indifferent to the plight of the poor. During the debate with Nikhil they cite several instances in which they admire zamindars who rule "with an iron hand." (130) Their attitude to the poor tends to be contemptuous and some of them refer to the underprivileged as "slaves by nature." (130) They gloat over Harish Kundu's strict rule in his estate, from which "you cannot ferret out a single ounce of foreign salt." (130) Kundu is also admired for his ruthlessness in dealing with a tenant who could not pay his rent. The tenant was forced to sell his young wife instead and gratify the zamindar's carnal desires. The students also praise Chakravati zamindar who puchased his starving tenant's silver ornaments for a measly five rupees. Men like Chakravati and Harish Kundu who rule with draconian measures become heroes in the minds of the impressionable young students. They chant, "if anybody can save our country it is these Kundus and these Chakravatis and their officials." (131)

Nikhil is shocked at such utterances and considers such attitudes as an offshoot of fear imposed by colonial rule. Replying to the quibbles of the students, Nikhil says: "The slavery that has entered into our very bones is breaking out, at this opportunity, as ghastly tyranny. You have been so used to submit to domination through fear, you have come to believe that to make others submit is a kind of religion. My fight shall be against this weakness, this atrocious cruelty!" (131)

Through the utterances and inner thoughts of Nikhil, Tagore conveys his concern that young minds are being misled by the rhetoric of political leaders and have lost humanitarian concerns. In another context, several decades later, Tharoor also expresses his consternation that authoritarian tendencies could appear attractive to the young in search of a livelihood as it promises quick solutions. Currently, Executive Assistant to the Secretary-General of the United Nations, Kofi Annan, Tharoor is worried that political contention could be considered a luxury in a developing country and "political freedom a dispensable distraction." (3) Way back in 1916, Tagore expressed similar fears. He was afraid that the swadeshi movement, being led by zamindars and upper caste Hindus would lead to mistrust, intolerance and fissiparous tendencies in the country.

In fact, Shormistha Panja, in her learned essay on Tagore, "The Elusive Mystery and Fluidity of Life," shows how Tagore became disillusioned with the Bengali swadeshi movement. She says that Tagore "particularly objected to the acts of arson and violence by the young Bengali terrorists." (108) Panja writes that the spate of killings and atmosphere of intolerance and violence dismayed Tagore: "The young revolutionary Khudiram Bose was hanged in 1908 for a failed attempt to kill the Muzaffarpur magistrate. Basant Biswas suffered a similar fate in 1913 for taking part in a conspiracy to the Viceroy Lord Hardinge in 1912." (108)

Tagore was frightened that the Indian tradition of peaceful coexistence was being ripped apart. He is more concerned with development of humanity. In his book *Nationalism*, he warns against the dangers of fanatical movements like the swadeshi uprising. Tagore says, "this nationalism is a cruel epidemic of evil that is sweeping over the human world of the present age and eating into its moral vitality." (36) He termed nationalism as a "fetish" and a "great menace," something that hypnotised races into an allusion of freedom. Hence Tagore was of the view that students should not boycott classes for the swadeshi cause.

Another instance that reveals both the class bias and the communal divide of the swadeshi movement was the sinking of Mirjan's boat. This is a case of victimisation against an underprivileged member of society in the guise of nationalism. Most of the boatmen refused to carry foreign goods but Mirjan, a Muslim, refused to comply with the order. Sandip orders his manager to sink thc boat. Mirjan is distressed that his boat worth Rs. 2,000 has been sunk and his means of livelihood destroyed. By such incidents the novelist shows that the swadeshi agitators did not care for sufferings of the underprivileged. The destruction of Mirjan's boat and burning some German shawls of a Muslim shopkeeper were all incidents that fuelled communal suspicion and later violence.

The contrasting views towards the Muslims also represent two differing viewpoints of nationalism in the book. Both Nikhil and Sandip raise this issue in the novel. Sandip takes the extreme view: "we shall never be able to ring them wholly around to our side. So they must be suppressed altogether and made to understand that we are the masters." (120) In contrast, the benevolent Nikhil says: "If the idea of a United India is a true one . . . the Mussalmans are a necessary part of it." (120) This view is in keeping with Tagore's ideas that nationalism should not be based on exclusiveness. He writes in *Nationalism*: "where the spirit of western nationalism prevails, the whole people is being taught from boyhood to foster hatreds and ambitions by all kinds of means—by the manufacture of half-truths and untruths in history by persistent misrepresentation of other races." (37) Sandip advocates subjugation of the Muslims for which he is willing to foster hatred and misrepresentations. Tagore is concerned that if Sandip's view prevails it would lead to alienation of the Muslims. By highlighting this vision of the future of India, Tagore has made his novel contemporaneous. It raises an important query about the inclusion of the demographic mass that exists in India. Should India continue with the pluralistic tradition or should a hegemonic national culture prevail, which Randhir Singh has called the "Hinduised Indian nationalism." (29)

Tagore is to be complimented for raising the contentious issue of minorities in his novel. It is a dilemma that is still unresolved. Shashi Tharoor in his book on India terms this imbroglio as, "The pluralism-versus-fundamentalism debate." Writing in 1997, Tharoor raises queries similar to that of Tagore, stating: "Is the secularism established in India's constitution, and now increasingly attacked as a westernised affectation, essential in a pluralist society, or should India like many Third World countries, find refuge in the assertion of its own religious identity." (4)

Tharoor stresses that the arguments about pluralism are not merely an academic debate but very relevant, as the choices made will determine the quality of life in sub-continent in the twenty-first century. So it can be seen that Tagore was very clairvoyant by raising the minority community issue in his novel. Tharoor's vision of India is like that of Tagore. Tharoor argues, "An India that denies itself to *some* Indians could end up being denied to *all* Indians." (5) He feels that variety is in itself integral to the idea of Indianness and that India is fundamentally a pluralist state. Tagore is also of the view that India is held together by strong but invisible threads. Tharoor feels that it is essential that India maintains its pluralist tradition as no other country in the world "embraces the extraordinary mixture of ethnic groups, the profusion of mutually incomprehensible languages, the varieties of topography and climate, the diversities of religions and cultural practises, and the range of levels of economic development." (7) So India the second most populous nation of earth with an estimated 1996 population of over 940 million and which stretches from 38 degress north latitude to 7 degrees above the equator is seen by Tharoor as an "ethnic melting pot" (11) or "a crucible of human striving." (16) Tharoor feels that "with diversity emerging from its geography (mountains to the north and north-west, water surrounding the rest) and inscribed in its history, India was made for pluralism." (13)

It is this vision of India, which Tagore tried to highlight through the views of Nikhil way back in 1915. Tagore is to be praised for his foresight. In fact, the eminent historian Sumit Sarkar points out that in the early years of the century, Tagore anticipated many future mass movements and problems that would confront India. In fact, Tagore's views on the Muslim question anticipates Mahatma Gandhi's ecumenist views. Both Gandhi and Tagore shunned the exclusionist revivalism practised by so many religions and cults in the contemporary world.

In the novel *The Home and the World*, we see that in many cases concerning the minorities and the poor, it is Nikhil's views which are practical and not that of the firebrand Sandip. Nikhil purchases Panchu's holdings to prevent Harish Kundu from enforcing eviction. When Bimala wants an old watchman dismissed for being rude to Sandip, he calms her down and does not dismiss the old man. He also takes practical steps to enable the poor Muslim traders continue their sale of goods. He explains to his wife Bimala why he is against the boycott of foreign goods in his market. He feels that such a ban will grievously hurt poor traders who were unable to financially afford the idealism of swadeshi. Hence as Nikhil tells his wife, such an imposition of swadeshi is like tyranny. Altruistic and benevolent Nikhil not only expresses concern but takes steps to alleviate the misery of the poor villagers.

This depiction of Nikhil is very autobiographical. Tagore donated his Nobel Prize money to help the underprivileged in society. He donated Rs. 110,000 of his Nobel Prize Money to the Shantiniketan School and the Agricultural Bank. The latter was set up to curb the exploitation of the poor peasants at the hands of the moneylenders and middlemen.

Nikhil and Sandip thus represent two differing outlooks on nationalism. The firebrand Sandip believes in the Machiavellian theory that the end justifies the means and uses even robbery and murder to further his cause. Nikhil in contrast is a highly idealised portrait of an enlightened humanist. There are other distinctive contrasts between these two friends. Sandip proclaims a type of nationalism which equates the country with a divine halo and with God. Such a depiction arouses feelings of jingoism and intolerance. Instead of human brotherhood, the followers of Sandip and his brand of nationalism look upon other countries as enemies. Nikhil objects to such extreme views.

Nikhil reflects Tagore's views on this contentious subject of ultra nationalism. Writing in his booklet, *Nationalism,* Tagore categorically stated that the country is not "greater than the ideals of humanity." (83) Tagore believes that a commercial or political basis for unity in a country is inadequate. He does not advocate the view that idolatry of the Nation is even better than reverence for God and humanity. Instead Tagore says: "I believe I have outgrown that teaching, and it is my conviction that my countrymen will truly gain their India by fighting against the education which teaches them that a country is greater than the ideals of humanity." (83)

It must be stressed that by such teachings, Tagore is not advocating a return to a mythical past. He candidly says: "I am not for thrusting off western civilisations and becoming segregated in our independence. Let us have a deep association." (85) He even welcomed the scientific achievements of the West. Tagore has often stressed that he is not against the idea of a nation but against the concept of aggressive nationalism. Instead he advocates the unity of races but on the strength of moral power, a spiritual unity and the "power to suffer for the truth." (87) Tagore uses the example of Indian history to justify his views. He says, "But in India, our difficulties being internal, our history has been the history of continual social adjustment and not that of organised power for defence and aggression." (48)

Thus in all types of crises, as regards dealing with the poor peasants or the small time Muslim traders, Tagore wants the spirit of social adjustment and moral power to prevail. Such a spirit is conveyed through Nikhil who even in the turbulent days of political agitation preaches the idea of nationalism, which is all-inclusive, spiritual and non-aggressive. In contrast Sandip's version of nationalism is based on exclusiveness, power, strength and if required even cruelty. In his vision of life, the great have to be cruel. Expostulating his views, Sandip says, "My theory of life makes me certain that the Great is cruel. To be just is for ordinary men—it is reserved for the great to be unjust." (78) Later Sandip also says that injustice, cruelty and subjugation are the only ways in which an individual or a nation can become successful. He says, "Successful injustice and genuine cruelty have been the only forces by which individual or nation has become millionaire or monarch." (79)

Sandip even practised what he preached. Once at a picnic with his followers, he saw a goat grazing in a field. To test his proteges, he asked them to cut off a leg of that goat and bring it to him. The young boys hesitated and so Sandip performed the act himself. It is such fanatical commitment to a cause that Sandip is advocating. In Sandip's vision of life, humanitarian feelings take a back seat. In the process of achieving targets or goals, like that of the swadeshi movement, moral values are inconsequential. For Sandip, moral values exist only for the lower classes and the ordinary men. He says, "let moral ideas remain merely for those poor anemic creatures of starved desire whose grasp is weak, . . . Nature surrenders herself but only to the robber." (49) It is the emergence of such fanaticism in the guise of the swadeshi movement or nationalism that worried Tagore. He wanted India to retain its spiritual distinctiveness even whilst making adjustments to the requirements of a modern material world.

Tagore is thus against rigid structures of nationalism. Speaking on the subject in Japan, Tagore had stressed that the East should influence the Western (European) model of nationalism, based on strength, free will and individualism. Such concepts have emerged through the centuries in writings ranging from the amoral treatise on statecraft of Niccolo Machiavelli (1469-1527) in the fifteenth and early sixteenth century to Friedrich Nietzsche (1844-1900) in the late nineteenth century. Speaking in Japan, Tagore says, "you must apply your eastern mind, spiritual strength, love of simplicity, recognition of social obligation in order to cut out a new path for this great unwieldy car of progress, shrieking out its loud discord as it runs." (22) So Tagore wants India to retain their spiritual identity and hence find solutions to the problems of race unity and surging nationalism.

Finally it must be said that in the depiction of nationalism and some other aspects, there are subtle differences between Tagore's novel and legendary director, the late Satyajit Ray's cinematic version of 1984. As Shormistha Panja indicates, "In Satyajit Ray's depiction one does not get the sense of a novel of ideas, of a serious examination of the nature of men and women, of love, of freedom, of marriage, of nationalism." In the novel Tagore tried to show the interaction between domestic life and public duties, between "an ideology imported from the West and given a local guise—swadeshi—and an inherent Indian tradition of toleration and peaceful existence of disparate even jarring elements." (109-10) In contrast, in Ray's film, the emphasis is more on just historical events and the Bimala-Sandip relationship.

The difference between the novel and the film is also the contrast between cinema text and novel text. Satyajit Ray in the depiction of the Bimala-Sandip relationship is clearcut whereas Tagore shows hesitancy. Tagore evoked passion subtly. Fantasy and romance is in the mind of Bimala. Satyajit Ray tends to trivialise the emotion by two rather forced kisses, which are not there in the novel. The kisses are inserted to suggest passion that Tagore evokes subtly by meaningful glances and touch of the hand. Again, in the film, there is a scene of Sandip barging into Nikhil and Bimala's bedroom and keeping Bimala's hairpin as a momento, which does not exist in the novel. The hairpin incident implies that there was greater physical intimacy between Bimala and Sandip than actually existed.

Historically, the swadeshi call for boycott of all English products, salt, sugar, clothes and woollens did not find support amongst the poor because they were substantially cheaper than Indian products. As Shirshendu Chakraborty, in his essay "In Search of an Elusive Freedom: History, Class and Gender in Tagore's *Ghare-Baire*," says that retail trade was mostly handled by Muslims who were amongst the poorer sections in Bengali society. It is this dilemma or contradiction, which the novel highlights effectively. The market in Nikhil's territory sells both Indian and British goods. Despite the threats and requests of the swadeshi activists. Nikhil refuses to remove British goods in the interests of his poor tenants. Failure irks the swadeshi agitators. They resort to subterfuge and duplicity and forcibly burn the foreign cloth being sold by the poor traders, causing the latter a lot of hardships.

So ultimately the novel can be read as a critique of the swadeshi movement which instead of inspiring nationalist sentiments, divides Indian society in terms of class and religion. In the novel the community and class division results in communal frenzy between Hindu and Muslim Bengalis. In these riots, Amulya, a young follower of Sandip dies and Nikhil is seriously injured. Tagore feels that such violence, hatred and divisiveness is an offshoot of fanatical nationalism or ostentatious patriotism concepts, which he abhors. The vision of India, that Tagore tries to convey in *The Home and the World* is that of Nikhil's Bharat which will include people like Panchu, the poor peasants, Muslim traders and the *bhadralok*—the educated, urban bourgeoisie.

Works Cited

Aijaz Ahmed, "A Century of Revolutions," *Frontline*, 4 February 2000, 123-26.

Sisir Ghose, *Rabindranath Tagore*. New Delhi: Sahitya Akademi, 1986, reprinted 1995.

Shirshendu Chakrabarti, "*In Search of an Elusive Freedom: History, Class and Gender in Tagore's Ghare-Baire*," in Panja, 99-106.

Subhas Mukhopadhyay, *Tagore without Bounds*. New Delhi: Sahitya Akademi, 1999.

Shormistha Panja, "The Elusive Mystery and Fluidity of Life and What Satyajit Ray Does to it: Ray's Sandipisation of Tagore's *Ghare-Baire*," in Shormistha Panja, ed., *Many Indias, Many*

Literatures: New Critical Essays. New Delhi: Worldview, 1999. 107-18.

Randhir Singh, "Of Nationalism in India Yesterday: Today and Tomorrow," *Mainstream*, 14 August 1999, pp. 27-36.

Rabindranath Tagore, *The Home and the World,* trans. Surendranath Tagore. New Delhi: Penguin, 1985.

Rabindranath Tagore, *Nationalism*. New Delhi: Rupa, 1992, first published by Macmillan in 1917.

Shashi Tharoor, *India from Independence to the Millennium.* New Delhi: Penguin, 1997.

NOTE

1. Central to Nietzsche's thought was the notion that with the development of the modern secular world, the traditional values (represented by Christianity) had lost their power in the lives of individuals, which he expressed in his infamous proclamation "God is dead." Modern efforts to ward off the threat of nihilism by transplanting transcendent authority into such ideals as, for example, reason or nature (as in the works of Thomas Hobbes and Jean-Jacques Rousseau respectively), were condemned by Nietzsche as the slavish urge of the "herd" or "mob." In contrast, he held aloft the tragic hero, who affirms life in the face of its meaninglessness. Against modern interpretations of progress as the realization of material goals, Nietzsche argued that the purpose of human life is to encourage the great individual (whom he calls the Übermensch-"overman" or "superman"). Such individuals will heroically construct meaning in the face of a paradoxically meaningless world—hence the subtitling of his work *The Twilight of the Idols* (1889; trans. 1968) as *How to Philosophize with a Hammer.* It is this creative will that for Nietzsche is the "will to power." He was convinced that traditional values represented a "slave morality," a morality created by weak and resentful individuals who encouraged such behaviour as gentleness and kindness because it served their interests. He claimed that new values could be created to replace the traditional ones, and his discussion of the possibility led to his concept of the overman.

   According to Nietzsche, the masses conform to tradition, whereas his ideal overman is secure, independent, and highly individualistic. The overman feels deeply, but his passions are rationally controlled. Concentrating on the real world, rather than on the rewards of the next world promised by religion, the overman affirms life, including the suffering and pain that accompany human existence. He is a creator of values, a creator of a "master morality" that reflects the strength and independence of one who is liberated from all values, except those that he deems valid.

Nietzsche maintained that all human behaviour is motivated by the will to power. In its positive sense, the will to power is not simply power over others, but the power over oneself that is necessary for creativity. Such power is manifested in the overman's independence, creativity, and originality. Although Nietzsche explicitly denied that any overmen had yet arisen, he mentions several individuals who could serve as models, including Socrates, Jesus Christ, Leonardo da Vinci, Michelangelo, Shakespeare, Goethe, Julius Caesar, and Napoleon.

The concept of the overman has often been interpreted as one that postulates a master-slave society and has been identified with totalitarian philosophies. Many scholars deny the connection and attribute it to misinterpretation of Nietzsche's work. The similarity between Nietzsche's works and Sandip's thought process is evident in Tagore's *The Home and the World* especially in the contemptuous attitude towards traditional value, the belief in the heroic individual and new codes of morality.

The Socio-Moral Metaphor: *The Home and the World*

PRADIP LAHIRI

Tagore's *The Home and the World* (1916) endeavours to blend realistic novel with the symbolic one. Its storyline runs along the emotional-intellectual reactions of three persons—Nikhil, the rich-class cultivated landlord husband; Bimala, his less cultured sensitive young homely wife; Nikhil's friend Sandip, the third sharp point of the triangle, a bohemian, so-called revolutionary. Generous Nikhil wants his homely wife Bimala to look at the outside world, cutting across her home confines. Bimala, introduced to Sandip by Nikhil himself, gets quickly drawn to the apparently fiery, robust personality—that which normally attracts women—of Sandip to the extent of allowing herself quite willingly to be seduced by him almost to the point of no return.

At the background, there looms large the mighty historical political event of the freedom movement oriented stormy Indian swadeshi movement, raging then in Bengal around the author. The significance of the novel is more obvious as ideological than socio-political.

Swadeshi (Be Indian, Buy Indian) raised its head as a politically conceived and augmented protest against the tyranny of the British rule in general, and the infamous Partition of Bengal in particular, brought about by Lord Curzon in 1905 (the Banga Bhanga). The movement also had an economic edge, with its insistence on the revival of the indigenous and small enterprises. Initially, Swadeshi raised the spirit of nationalism, and remained capped within the peaceful orbit of a strong vociferous protest against the ogre of an oppressive foreign yoke. By degrees, it got diluted with unwholesome terrorist outfits mushroomed in different parts of Bengal, with the motivation of using violence against the White oppressors. What also happened was that a section of the Swadeshi enthusiasts participated more in destroying foreign-made articles than in the manufacture of indigenous usables instead. These unmethodical, violent, destructive activities failed to elicit any effective public appreciation, especially owing to the fact that somewhere behind these inchoate violent exercises—although grown out of some patriotic zeal—a shadow of an evil impulse for greed and anarchy was cast. Intelligent, sensitive, educated and cultured as they were, though economically distressed and politically non-plussed, the Indian middle-class as well as the well-to-do segment did not miss noticing this apparition. They were in a dilemma, felt annoyed and fought shy.

Can it be said that Tagore was torn between his ever-cherished Sufi idealism, and the whirlwind of happenings around him? Was he facing the ordeal of sitting in judgement over the Upanishad inculcated "Shreya" and "Preya"? Tagore's equipoise mind had always an Eastern calm and philosophic orientation which went in avidly for the cosmos, the cosmic, the central, the eternal—never ever reconciling with chaos, peripheral and the ephemeral. With his stable convictions and a cultivated saintly sangfroid derived from the Upanishads, in *The Home and the World*, Tagore sought to present his literary brief before his readers, detailing and enunciating, but never dove-tailing the two sides of the raging controversy—to float, or to sink, with the Swadeshi, or to retrace steps to question, to examine. Tagore the seer, the ever-romantic, had never been satisfied with 'here and now.' For him, the quest was for something afar, away in some distant, unknown territory, to be arrived at through the deep-felt perception of an inner reality, an esoteric truthful conviction.

As a socio-political novel, *The Home and the World* seems to make a sharp distinction between rival, dichotomised impulses. If Nikhil stands to represent a scrupulous passion for constructive Swadeshi activities, Sandip having dissimilar character traits, lays bare the acts of a dangerous stimulant bringing out the darker aspect of mankind—the greed, the treachery, the lust, rather cheap excitement and a destructive propensity—lying in constant wait behind the apparently innocent, patriotic movement.

Those who consider the novel as a rich allegory, or a complex metaphor, may as well associate Nikhil with the Indian old guards protecting values; Bimala with the confused state of the masses at a transitional juncture; while Sandip can be viewed as a representative of those ultra-moderns who were infatuated by Europe's continuous urge for action, wrought through rapid changes in the West, considerably permeating the gentle tenor of a quiet meditative way of Indian life.

Swadeshi movement is not what really matters in *The Home and the World* at the conceptual level. On the contrary, it works as a catalyst to bring about the chemical reaction between the couple Nikhil and Bimala caught in the net of the psychological conflict, involving the home on the one hand, and the world on the other. For Bimala, her husband's highly appreciable homely image does not get reflected against the mirror of the world, as Bimala was getting to know the external world, when in her own words "Swadeshi storm reached my blood," (27) especially under the influence of the glitter and glamour of Sandip's turbulent presence and his wanton, wayward personality. Nikhil stands for the home and Sandip for its antithesis, the world. Swadeshi has been used as an outlet through which a cloistered wife of a conventional household can suddenly tear herself from the moorings of a sheltered domestic existence, and float adrift in the lagoon of the excitement of an agitation.

The Home and the World is replete with political observations and commentaries—not in the nature of a propaganda—which are significant if they help to reveal the workings of the minds of two men and one woman. The actual theme lies in the responsibilities, trials and adjustments which Nikhil has to make as a result of his desire to found his relationship with his wife Bimala on the pedestal of truth. Bimala's mind-set started changing under the impact of the Swadeshi-generated passion—just at this point of time, Bimala encounters Sandip, the firebrand nationalist, who thinks, feels and acts very differently from her consort Nikhil with whom she is tied by the bonds of a moralistic, conventional, sacrosanct marriage, which in those days sternly ruled out any association with any other man in opposition to the husband, let alone physical proximity or direct interaction. Tagore was concerned with the profound identity crisis in the colonial India of the given period, from which the males agonisingly suffered. Womenfolk, nonetheless, were in an obvious quandary as regards their self, socio-political situation, moral moorings and personal identity. What was at stake was the subjugation of the individual self of a wife, a woman, and the negation of the 'self' cutting across the 'sex' factor.

In this deep psychedelic matrix and against the spectrum of the strong current of diversified happenings, there arose a subjective personal problem of re-defining and re-adjusting man's relation with woman. The applecart of the male complacency got upset. Until a man could first convince himself over the restitution of his self-respect, how could he be a hero in the eyes of his wife?

What Tagore wanted to put forward in the novel was how an exposure of the outer world could make a home-spun woman transformed in many respects, and thereby could as well erode and threaten the structure of the conservative households. As a result, the entire nature, the volume, the verve and the rhythm of a very personal husband-wife relationship had to undergo a drastic change. Ultimately, Tagore was convinced that various humiliations to womanhood in the traditional Hindu households, not to speak of other religious communities, were no less just and degrading than the racial ignominy of the menfolk in the colonial system of working in the outer ritual ideology. Bimala in *The Home and the World* submitted to no coercion of any sort, but to a moral and perhaps spiritual ideology. Even in a rich and adequately comfortable household, a woman like Bimala started finding it hard not to feel frustrated, and not to suffer from an acute sense of non-fulfilment. A loneliness at an intangible emotional sphere started stalking her psyche. Her idolized husband, more often than not, failed to come up to complement or supplement this sense of isolation in her reflective midriff, owing to their ordinary or cowardly over-inflated or arrogant, pretentious or indifferent, bland or dumb nature. A sense of stifled existential agony was almost imperceptibly surfacing.

At a later stage, both Nayantara Sahgal and Anita Desai, the two illustrious Indian English authors, choosing the background of a newly independent India, did try to reveal this sense of an acute isolation and crisis of identity of the Indian women.

Tagore wanted to show that women as independent entities were not being understood, and that their desires, expectations and inchoate needs had to remain unexpressed. In his *Nasta Neer* (Broken Home, 1891), Tagore took up this issue.

However, as a corollary, such an abrupt exposure with the external world—since what happened was that women, especially in the upper echelons of the educated society started getting exposure in an increasing number to be acquainted with the outer world of activities, of encounters with ideas and ideologies and assorted experiences—had several pitfalls and snares of illusions, as boldly underscored in *The Home and the World*, potential enough to delude and catch an inexperienced woman almost unawares in an unsure, dangerous and menacing extra-marital affairs, threatening to severely ruining the home-front, as well as the moral identity of a woman.

In his *Chitrangada* (1892), Tagore wanted to work out a true relationship between man and woman, pointing out that there was nothing to be achieved by a sense of 'right' (*Adhikar*), but it is possible to build a complementary partnership founded on mutual respectful understanding. The Manipur princess in *Chitrangada* demanded from Arjuna, the brave third Pandava, such a partnership which, having extended the home front, opens out into the external world. She, in one of her dignified utterances proclaimed that as a woman, she would like to be her man's comrade in weal and woe, to be his close associate in difficult enterprises, trials and tribulations, to be his follower and companion in adventures, and to be a co-sharer of his anxious disturbing moments.

However, the moralist Tagore, at the very end of *The Home and the World*, saved Bimala from immorality and spiritual fall, and brought her back to Nikhil and the home—perhaps a reformed one, a mature woman who would see herself in the light of her renovated, newly discovered self and soul, in ascertaining her 'position' vis-a-vis her husband Nikhil in the home, and in relation to the world outside.

Convergence of Ideologies: Consideration of *Swadeshi* in *The Home and the World* in the Light of Gandhi's *Hind Swaraj*

SUBHASH CHANDRA

A large part of the critical response to *The Home and the World* focuses on the woman question, especially in relation to Bimala's exposure to the world outside home and her temporary 'politico-sexual' attraction to Sandip, the fiery, militant exponent of *swadeshi*. This is just as well because the novel written as it was in 1916 (serialized in a Bengali journal *Sabujpatra* in 1915-16) constitutes a radical feminist statement at a time when the second wave of feminism was at least four and half decades away and the Indian society was largely conservative in the matter of positioning of women. Another point of debate in the criticism of this book concerns the binary of tradition and modernity—Nikhilesh and Sandip—symbolizing the two concepts respectively. While on the issue of woman's place in society, Tagore is given credit for presenting a radical viewpoint (though some critics censure him for bringing Bimala back into the four walls of home and making her experience guilt and remorse), on the question of *swadeshi*, he is castigated for his pro-colonial, bourgeois views which favoured statis. George Lukacs's condemnation of Tagore, bordering on bitter vituperation (to which I would revert later in the paper) forms an important part in the denunciatory stance adopted by some critics towards Tagore. Even though Tagore and Gandhi, the two towering figures of the early twentieth century, were contemporaries and were in touch with each other (they exchanged letters, valued each other's opinions and observations on issues of national importance), not much attention has been paid to the influence of Gandhi on Tagore's thinking, as reflected in his fictional and non-fictional writings. The intention of the present paper is precisely to do this.

To begin with, I would like to explain the *swadeshi* movement and its ramification. *Swadeshi* meant literally things pertaining to one's own country. It was a many-faceted national movement which arose as a reaction to the partition of Bengal in 1905 effected by Lord Curzon, the then Viceroy. (The partition was revoked in 1911). The partition divided the Province of Bengal into two provinces: (i) West Bengal, Bihar and Orissa with Hindu majority, and (ii) East Bengal and Assam with a Muslim majority. An immediate political fall-out of the partition was that until then it was thought that for the redress of grievances, Indians must approach the throne and if the grievance was not redressed, people realized that petitions must be backed up by force and that they must be prepared for suffering. This was the feeling at the back of the *swadeshi* movement. At the economic level, the movement involved the boycott of British goods, aiming to stop their imports. At the educational level, it founded national educational institutions in Calcutta. Aurobindo Ghose resigned in 1906 from his post at Baroda College and joined as professor of history and political science, in addition to assuming responsibilities of the Principal of Bengal National College in Calcutta. As R.C. Majumdar tells us, at the political level, the movement led to resignations from legislative councils. (33-64) Gandhi's comments on the *swadeshi* movement in 1905 were: "The movement in Bengal for the use of swadeshi goods is much like the Russian movement," (1958: 5, 132) and in 1907 he compared the movement of *Sinn Fein*, which "literally translated into Gujarati, means exactly our *Swadeshi* movement." (1958: 7, 213)

Gandhi's elaborate exposition of *swadeshi* in his *The Collected Works* is relevant for my purpose of responding to the movement as it is represented in the novel. He writes:

> No cause for unhappiness would remain if *Swadeshi* were to replace everything foreign. We can easily attain happi-

> ness if we exert ourselves to that and during the year that has just commenced. *Swadeshi* carries a great and profound meaning. It does not mean merely the use of what is produced in one's own country. That meaning is certainly there in *swadeshi*. But there is another meaning implied in it which is far greater and much more important. *Swadeshi* means reliance on our own strength. We should also know what we mean by 'reliance on our strength.' 'Our strength' means the strength of our body, our mind and our soul. From among these, on which should we depend? The answer is brief. The soul is supreme, and therefore soul-force is the foundation on which man must build. Passive resistance or *satyagraha* is a mode of fighting which depends on such force. That, then is the only real key (to success) for the Indians. (1958: 9, 118)

It is noteworthy that Gandhi stressed the 'soul-force' (*satyagraha*) for making *swadeshi* a success—coercion, terrorism and violence do not form part of the movement. The critique which the novel mounts on the *swadeshi* movement, heralded by Sandip, parallels Tagore's own distrust and sharp criticism of the movement. According to him, fanatic nationalism contained certain dangers, which could eventually prove inimical to the marginalized sections of society. He objected to the acts of violence and arson by the young Bengali terrorists. Tagore categorically refused permission to young school and college students to join *swadeshi* movement at the cost of their studies. He told a friend that he was frightened of the abstraction that was nationalism. In his book, *Nationalism*, Tagore called nationalism a "fetish" and a "great menace," something that hypnotized allegedly free races into an illusion of freedom. (1955: 58-79) Tagore is critical of nationalism in his other fictive writings as well: *Gora* and *Char Adhyay* are two other examples, in addition to *Ghare Baire*, in which, as Shirshendu Chakrabarti points out, Tagore "exposes the class bias and the servile greed for power concealed in such nationalism." (1999: 100) Chakrabarti goes on to observe: "*Bhadralok* (middle class) militancy is correctly shown to be ineffective on the colonial rulers, and its targets are, ironically enough, the poor and vulnerable sections of society. In fact, Tagore suggests an insidious similarity between the colonial master and *Bhadralok* subject." (100) The similarity comes through the colonial master's selfishness, which excluded the interests of the ruled country, and the narrow egotism of Sandip, the prime mover and champion of *swadeṣhi*, for whom all that matters is his own success (through the ostensible success of the movement he is attempting to spread) and his own comfort, for he cannot live the life of an ordinary man, the life of simplicity and asceticism—he regards himself above the followers he is leading and the masses he is trying to galvanize into action against the colonial masters. The second point of similarity between *swadeshi* movement and the British colonialism was the coercive force which the two employed to implement their agendas in complete disregard of the suffering it caused to people. One does not have to go into details of the force exerted by the British masters, but it would be pertinent to mention the abrasive and aggressive attitude of Sandip and his cohorts in dealing with poor traders who found it difficult to fall in line with the *diktats* issued by Sandip, because it meant losing their livelihood. Let us, first of all, trace the type of followers Sandip attracted. We are told: "A band of young fellows of the locality attached themselves to him, some even who had been known as a disgrace to the village." (94) Nikhil's argument, offered to the agitated students (some of whom had been on scholarships being given by him) who demanded he remove the foreign goods from his *Shuksayar* market, was: "the loss would fall on the poor traders and their customers, not on me." (101) That the movement contained a fanatic streak and abstract high idealism, divorced from the humanity of the humans and their day-to-day struggle for survival is brought out by Chandranath Babu's firm rejoinder to the militant students: "You may do as you please to work off you irritation, to keep up your fanaticism. You are well off, you need not mind the cost. The poor do not want to stand in your way, but you insist on their submitting to your compulsion. As it is, every moment of theirs is a life-and-death struggle for a bare living, you cannot even imagine the difference a few pice means to them—so little have you in common. You have spent your whole past in a superior compartment, and now you come down to use them as tools for the wreaking of your wrath. I call it cowardly." (101-2)

The tyranny of the movement rubs off poor Panchu whose bundle of foreign cloth is burned to ashes which are put to a histrionic use by Sandip: he picks up the ashes and declares: "This is the first funeral pyre lighted by your village in celebration of the last rites of foreign commerce. These are sacred ashes. Smear yourselves with them in token of your *Swadeshi* vow." (104) The militancy and aggressiveness of the movement is stressed by Sandip who tells Amulya that if those whose foreign goods are confiscated take the matter to the law, their granaries must be burned in retaliation. The *swadeshi* proponents do not stop short of depriving a poor boatman, Mirjan, of his only source of livelihood by stealthily sinking his boat just because he does not fall in line and refuses their command not to ferry foreign goods. The lack of morality, practised for the sake of the movement, is condensed in Sandip's words who goes to Bimala to ask for money: "by hook or by crook, we must have it [money]." "By hook or by crook" becomes the quintessence of the *swadeshi* movement. This deviousness and lack of morality is paralleled by Sandip's inner degeneration who does not feel any moral compunction in attempting to seduce the wife of his close friend, whose hospitality he is enjoying as guest. What Tagore seems to be suggesting is that Sandip's inner degeneration cannot be instrumental in bringing about anything worthwhile. Just as Sandip is a fake, so is the movement he is spearheading—*swadeshi*, as Sandip perceives it, does not at all mean the good of all. *Swadeshi* coerces and tyrannizes over the poor, and excludes Muslims from the ambit of fruits of independence, as and when it is won by India.

It would be pertinent here to know Gandhi's thinking on the relation between the purity of inner self and political action and the use of violence but before that I would like to revert to Lukacs's criticism of Tagore. His denunciation of Tagore's attitude to *swadeshi*, and the struggle for the Indian freedom movement is intensely rabid. He devalues the Nobel Prize for Literature conferred on Tagore: "The English bourgeoisie has reasons of its own for rewarding Mr. Tagore with fame and riches (the Nobel Prize); *it is repaying its intellectual agent in the struggle against Indian freedom movement.*" (9) What Lukacs does not seem to know is that Tagore was a vocal opponent of the partition of Bengal. At a huge meeting held in Calcutta's Town Hall, he proposed that the day of partition, October 1905, be observed as a symbolic *rakhi* day to mark the brotherhood of all Bengalis. He tied *rakhis* around the wrists of Muslim ostlers and *mullahs* in the mosque at Chitpur. He collected an impressive sum of Rs. 5,000 for the National Fund. He composed about twenty three patriotic songs including the famous "Jodi Tor Dak Shune Keu Na Ashe Tobe Aikla Cholo Re." (If no one responds to your call, walk alone) and "Banglar Mati, Banglar Jol" (Bengal's earth, Bengal's water). It was only when he found young Bengali terrorists indulging in acts of arson and violence that he became disillusioned with the Bengal *swadeshi* movement. The novel dramatizes the rejection of *swadeshi* precisely on account of its terrorist dimension and its indifference to the poor.

Gandhi's thinking runs parallel to Tagore's as far as the connection between self-realization and politics is concerned. According to Gandhi, the two may not be radically separated. Inner change within the individual, in fact, has to constitute the starting point of outer change which he wishes to bring about in society. Tagore makes it clear in the novel that Sandip, with his self-seeking acquisitiveness and deceit, cannot become the instrument of social regeneration. It is important to note that the modern social scientists ignore the connection between the inner self-realization and politics, but Gandhi reinstates it into political philosophy. George Gatlin shows correct understanding of Gandhi on this point when he says that *Hind Swaraj* "teaches that project of outer transformation ought to begin with the inner-transformation of the moral agent." (1950) Anthony J. Parel, in his introduction to *Hind Swaraj* also stresses the same point when he observes: "*Hind Swaraj* besides being a dialogue on *swaraj* is an intensely 'spiritual' and intensely 'practical' book, one that teaches that there is a link between inner life and outer achievement, that individual regeneration and national regeneration constitute one continuum. However difficult the task of bringing about outer transformation may appear to be, there is always something that the concerned individual can do, and that is to bring about, his or her inner transformation." (1997: lxii) Tagore seems to attribute the failure of *swadeshi* movement in *Shuksayar* to Sandip's complete lack of moral values. Sandip's humiliation at the hands of Bimala (who was his admirer for some time), the Hindu-Muslim riots which the movement foments and the consequent disharmony and violence in an otherwise peaceful *Shuksayar* society are meant to be considered as pointers that no movement can succeed without the inner purity of the self of those who lead it.

I would like to point out another significant parallel between Gandhi's view on violence and militancy as contained in *Hind Swaraj* and Tagore's stance on this issue in *The Home and the World*. Panchu's fear of the *swadeshi* supporters exemplifies the brutality and the violence inherent in the movement: "They will burn down my house, sir, children and all," he tells Nikhil, who feels shocked at the burning of Panchu's bundle of foreign cloth. The ruthless violence being perpetrated by the proponents of *swadeshi* is exhibited in the letter to Nikhil, symbolically written in blood-red ink, informing him of the strict action taken against the recalcitrant zamindars. In Nikhil's words: "Then comes a letter in blood-red ink, giving a list of the traitorous *zamindars* whose treasuries have been burnt down because of their failing to support the cause. 'Holy Fire,' it goes on to say 'has been aroused to its sacred function of purifying the country.'" (128) The letter goes on to threaten: "and other agencies are also at work to see that those who are not true sons of the motherland do cease to encumber her lap." (129) I would like to refer to Gandhi's response to the ideology of political terrorism adopted by the expatriates. *Hind Swaraj* was written in order to emphasize that the expatriates were pursuing "a suicidal policy." Gandhi recalled how on his 1909 visit to London he had come into contact with Indian anarchists there, and how he had wanted to write a book in answer to the Indian school of violence: "I felt that violence was no remedy for India's ills, and that her civilization required the use of a different and higher weapon for self-protection." (1958, 19:277)

Hind Swaraj was published in 1909 and *The Home and The World* in 1916. I have not come across a specific mention that Tagore read *Hind Swaraj* to assimilate its tenets (it cannot be ruled out, though), but it is reasonable to assume that he was familiar with the book and the ideas it contained. And since he held Gandhi in great esteem and valued his views on issues of importance, he interwove Gandhian ideas into the texture of the novel.

Works Cited

Catlin, George. *In the Path of Mahatma Gandhi*. Chicago, 1950.

Chakrabarty, Shirshendu. "In Search of an Illusive Freedom: History, Class and Gender in Tagore's *Ghare-Baire*," in Shormishtha Panja, ed. *Many Indias, Many Literatures*. New Delhi: Worldview, 1999, pp. 99-106.

Gandhi, Mahatma. *The Collected Works*. Ahmedabad: Navajivan, 1958.

_____. *Hind Swaraj*, ed. Anthony J. Parel. Cambridge: University Press, 1997.

Lukacs, George. *Reviews and Articles* from Die rote Fahne. Trans. Peter Palmer. London: Merlin Press, 1983.

Majumdar, R.C. *History of the Freedom Movement in India*. 2 vols. Calcutta, 1975.

Tagore, Rabindranath. *Nationalism*. 1955; New Delhi: Rupa, 1992.

_____. *The Home and the World*. New Delhi: Penguin, 1985.

The Home and the World: A Study in the Themes

SAVITRI TRIPATHI

Tagore is a glorious legend in the literary field in addition to his talents and gifts as poet, playwright, philoshoper, painter, composer, novelist, short story writer, educationist, cultural hero and a junction point of Indian and foreign traditions. He is the most outstanding name in modern Bengali literature and gained for modern India a place in the world literary scene. The Goddess of Fine Arts showered upon him a special blessing at the tender age of eight.

Tagore's literary genius is incomparable. The important aspects of his genius are the variety and versatility of his inexhaustible writings. Apart from these, he was a great humanist and universalist and taught a whole generation of the country to be humanist, not vaguely but by creating in his novels those characters, those human beings, who are so real in their weaknesses. He is more than a philosophical humanist. He believed in one world and in the internal vision of man evolving into the idea of Vishwa-Manava. Tagore's humanism was in fact born of his belief in spiritualism and, paradoxical though it may appear, he was a staunch humanist because he was a profound spiritualist. He was born in the Upanishadic atmosphere of his family. To him the entire world is manifestation of God. The best in the most tangible expression of Tagore's humanism is to be found in his novels. Though nearly each of his novels overflows with the profound love for earth and humanity but his four novels *Gora, Chaturanga, The Home and the World* (*Ghare Baire*) and *Char Adhyay* (*Four Chapters*), protest against all kinds of barriers of family, caste, rituals, the sects, groups, party, nation etc. that divide men and dwarf their personalities.

The novel *The Home and the World,* set on a Bengali zamindar's estate in 1908, has several themes. It deals with the humanism of Tagore and conflicts of the age. It also deals with the social and psychological problems. The novel brings out the triangular relationship involving Nikhil, Bimala and Sandip. The theme of the novel, based on the Swadeshi movement, activates and complicates the relationship between the characters introduced in the novel highlighting the tension and conflict between the home and the world. The Swadeshi movement, so far as Tagore was concerned, meant economic and social emancipation. Tagore had all along supported the Swadeshi movement as it sought to promote the goods of the country. It is for this reason that the novel evoked much interest in the world at large. The issue that it raised was relevant to the situation prevailing in the country. But the novel is not an investigation of the Swadeshi movement as Bhabani Bhattacharya has rightly remarked: "It is human interest in *The Home and the World* that mainly counts. The characters are no pawns in the hands of history, even if they are good symbols."[1]

Nikhil's idea of freedom, self-government and constructive leadership is in complete accord with Tagore's own vision of the struggle for independence. He is presented as a patriot to the core of his heart. He did all he could to encourage the Swadeshi production of goods in his estates, though success did not embrace him.

Sandip, on the other hand, is opposite to Nikhil. He is busy in achieving personal power. He is seen going about inflaming the people with the cult of "Bande Mataram" and the conflict of the freedom by force. Nikhil knows that what Sandip is doing will not have impact on common man.

Nikhil is a humanist who arranges for his wife's English education. He goes to the extent of introducing her to modern ways of life. In fact, he wants her to be in tune with the spirit of the age. It is with this view that he goes about encouraging his wife to step into the larger world. Bimala does not find in her husband's concept of Swadeshi that force and fire which is noticeable in the pronouncements of Sandip. It is because of this that her husbands's dull and watery Swadeshi does not appeal to her. It is at this crucial point in the story that Tagore brings Swadeshi into the picture. His fiery eloquence simply holds Bimala spell-bound, Bimala's mistaken ideas of being the "Shakti of the Motherland" is exploited to the maximum by Sandip. He leaves no stone unturned to keep Bimala in good humour. He calls her the 'Queen Bee' of the Swadeshi workers. She feels greatly flattered when she is told by Sandip that the entire country is in her hands. Bimala writes in her diary:

> So long I had been like a small river at the border of a village. My rhythm and my language were different from what they are now. But the tide came up from the sea, and my breast heaved. My banks gave way and then great drum beats of the sea waves echoed in my mad current. I could not understand the meaning of that sound in my blood.[2]

Nikhil is fully alive to the turn of the situation but does nothing to disturb the peace of the atmosphere. He is aware of Bimala's growing infatuation but does not think it proper to intervene. He entertains the idea that truth will dawn upon Bimala and prevent her from being exploited by Sandip.

At the end of the novel, Bimala realizes the truth and repents whole-heartedly. Nikhil forgives her and is ready to accept her but their reunion does not last long. Nikhil is seriously injured in his attempt to save the neighbouring women who have been tortured in communal riots. It is with Bimala's disconsolate look at the injured Nikhil that the novel comes to an end. Thus Tagore highlights the internal conflict which ultimately leads to the discovery of self in Bimala.

Nikhil, a staunch believer in the Swadeshi Movement, however, is totally opposed to narrow-minded patriotism and violence of any kind. Though a gentle and generous man, he is very firm in his denunciation of violence or the use of force. Condemning Sandip's narrow minded nationalism as a wicked legacy of the western military style, he tells him: "To tyrannize for the country is to tyrannize over the country." (142)

Nikhil is a supporter of humanity, and when he finds that Sandip's narrow vision makes him disregard the Mohammedans in the country, he remarks: "If the India of a united India is a true one, Mussalmans are the necessary part of it." (158)

Tagore's humanism is visible in his awareness of life and problems of the people around him. For him, worship of man is worship of God. As Sandip says: "But my powers are limited so my worship of humanity is continued in the worship of my country." (37) Nikhil remarks: "I have nothing against your worship as such, but how is it you propose to conduct your worship of god by hating other countries in which He is equally manifest?" (37)

Tagore was worshipper of humanity. For him God manifests himself both in man and in country. There is no difference between man and man. Nikhil's liberalism and humanism make him tolerate Sandip's presence in house for some months, but when he finds his followers in their fervid enthusiasm for the Swadeshi movement inflicting tortures on his poor peasants and creating a gulf between Hindus and Muslims, he asks him to leave his house and village. His wife Bimala, now completely disillusioned about Sandip's narrow-minded nationalism, also approves her husband's action. Sandip is, therefore, left with no alternative but to leave them.

The Home and the World presents a combination of two kinds of fiction. It is a cross between the realistic novel such as *Gora* and the symbolist novel such as the *Broken Ties*. It portrays the emotional and intellectual reaction of three sensitive persons—Nikhil, Bimala and Sandip—against the mighty political movement of Swadeshi which took Bengal by storm in the early years of the twentieth century. As a political social novel, it makes a sharp distinction between two rival impulses, the pure passion for constructive work and the greed and destructive energy. Nikhil worships nothing but truth which is greater than the country; for Sandip, the ideal is tolerable only when it is a means to the attainment of the real. Bimala is torn between these two persons of opposing ideals.

Nikhil, like a real Karma yogi, believes only in truth and neither adopts foul means to get freedom nor likes Sandip's way of getting freedom. For Nikhil, there is no difference between man and man and between country and country. He believes in universal brotherhood. There is remarkable difference between the eastern and western concepts of the nature of man. According to Christian faith, man is sinful and guilty and so needs salvation. On the other hand, according to the Vedantic view, man is good virtually because the Infinite is potentially present in him, ever guiding his actions on earth.

Nikhil's passion for absolute truth reminds us of the sages of ancient India. Tagore, like a preacher of the Upanishadic days, preaches us to be truthful and kind. He writes in Sadhana: "The writer has been brought up in a family where texts of the *Upanishads* are used in daily worship and he has had before him the example of his father who lived his long life in the closest communion with God, while not neglecting his duties to the world."

Tagore's close association with Maharshi Devendranath, whose life was dedicated to principles of the *Upanishads*, helped to develop in him a deep and profound intimacy with the *Upanishads*. He was born with a bent of mind which was intrinsically in perfect tune with the spirit of the *Upanishads*. Tagore writes: "To me the verses of the *Upanishads* and the teaching of Buddha have ever been things of the spirit, and therefore endowed with boundless vital growth, and I have used them both in my preaching."[4]

The novel also deals with psychological conflict, the personal drama of husband and wife, known to each other both at home and in the world. Bimala, Nikhil's wife, an ordinary, domesticated type who becomes extraordinary when her passion and her vanity are aroused—a real and convincing character. Nikhil, a loving husband, desires that his relationship with his wife be set up on the freedom of love, in order to make it abiding. This can be done when she comes out of the seclusion of the home and mingles freely with the outside world.

The novel has raised the problem of married life. Marriage is an external bondage, to keep together souls that cannot be alike. In the novel, each of the three major characters reveals his or her own thoughts in a diary and has his or her own method to deal with the problems. Nikhil has his own method of approach and creates his own problems. He does not want to make his wife Bimala a puppet in his hands. He does not impose anything of his own on her but wants that she should know the larger world. In a Bengali household those days, the wife belonged entirely to the home; it was very difficult to give her freedom, that is realized in the outside world. By introducing Swadeshi movement in this story, Tagore provides an opportunity to Bimala to come out of the house. This shows the liberal outlook of Nikhil towards his wife Bimala. But Sandeep, the new satanic nationalist leader, sweeps Bimala into his fold, takes her out of home into the world. This had been her husband Nikhilesh's dearest desire, only it is fulfilled in contrary ways. Bimala who takes undue advantage of her husband's liberal outlook, is under the spell of Sandip's sensual vitality. Sandip, a champion of greed, is showy. Once when Bimala says: "I would make my country a person and call her mother, Goddess Durga," (39-40) Sandip shouts 'Hurrah!' but the next moment he corrects and cries: "Bande Mataram!" Seeing his showy temperament, a shadow of pain passes on the face of Nikhil and he says to Bimala: "Neither am I divine: I am human and therefore I dare not permit the evil which is in me to be exaggerated into an image of my country, never—never!" (40)

Sandip is not prepared to recognize any moral ideal that may stand in the way of immediate success, for him ideals are mere illusions. He wants to break all the walls which come in the way of his success. He is very far from idealism of Nikhil as the dark moon from the full. He flatters Bimala and calls her the incarnation of 'Shakti' but Bimala soon discovers that behind the sparkle of Sandip's brilliance, there is cowardice and meanness and ultimately she has utter disgust for Sandip.

It is not only the problem of Sandip and Bimala but it is the problem of the society in which we live. We find that the problem of Nikhil and Bimala is deeper. Nikhil has been married to Bimala for nine years and proved himself a good husband. He does not impose on her the restrictions of society but when Bimala gets infatuated by Sandip and tension between them becomes acute, he tells her that she is free: "To try to keep Bimala as a garland round my neck would have meant keeping a weight hanging over my heart." (178)

The novel also has autobiographical touches. It is noteworthy that Nikhil in the crisis of his life hears true voice of his sister-in-law and recalls the days of boyhood: "At last I would hear the true voice of home. The Bara Rani came into our house as its bridge, when I was only six years old. We have played together, through the drowsy afternoons in a corner of the roof-terrace." (258)

His sister-in-law had been his friend and playmate of his boyhood days. He compares Bimala and his poor unfortunate, widowed and childless sister-in-law. He has sympathy for his sister-in-law but Bimala could not tolerate it although she has been provided with all the facilities of life and is loved by Nikhil. The words of Nikhil used for Bimala show his deep love for her. "When I came out, I found Bimala sitting on the floor outside. Could this be my Bimala of old, my proud, sensitive Bimal?" (263) He again says: "She came hesitatingly, barefoot, with a white shawl over head. I had never seen my Bimal like this before." (266)

The Home and the World is considered to be one of Tagore's greatest novels. It describes the various distinctions between men and women belonging to the old aristocratic feudal traditions. The novel however speaks of the social traditions of Bengal at the time of its partition. The atmosphere of the novel is tense, reflecting the tension of the period it depicts. Tagore is for a happy blend of the old and the new, the East and the West, the Home and the World, tradition and science in this realistic novel.

Although the novel is a poet's manifesto, it is equally a testament of Gandhi's philosophy of non-violence, love and truth. When we read the novel we feel how akin Tagore was to Gandhi in spirit, whatever the seeming difference in their ways.

In this way the novel that lays emphasis on the importance of man and human values above every thing else gives Tagore a unique place in Indian English literature. What Wordsworth did for England and Whitman for America, the same Tagore did for India.

NOTES

1. Bhabani Bhattacharya, "Tagore as a Novelist," *Rabindranath Tagore* (New Delhi: Sahitya Akademi, 1961), p. 99.
2. R.N. Tagore, *The Home and the World* (Macmillan India, 1985), p. 56.
3. R.N. Tagore, "Preface" *Sadhana* (Macmillan India, 1988), p. 7.
4. *Ibid* p. 8.

